MW00945914

FINDING
YOUR
SPIRITUAL
TRUTH

FINDING YOUR YOUR SPIRITUAL TRUTH

PROPHETESS BEULYTA GREEN DOYLE

XULON PRESS ELITE

Xulon Press Elite
2301 Lucien Way #415
Maitland, FL 32751
407.339.4217
www.xulonpress.com

© 2021 by Prophetess Beulyta Doyle

All rights reserved solely by the author. The author guarantees all contents are original and do not infringe upon the legal rights of any other person or work. No part of this book may be reproduced in any form without the permission of the author. The views expressed in this book are not necessarily those of the publisher.

Unless otherwise indicated, Scripture quotations taken from the New American Standard Bible (NASB). Copyright © 1960, 1962, 1963, 1968, 1971, 1972, 1973, 1975, 1977, 1995 by The Lockman Foundation. Used by permission. All rights reserved.

Scripture quotations taken from the New King James Version (NKJV). Copyright © 1982 by Thomas Nelson, Inc. Used by permission. All rights reserved.

Scripture quotations taken from the King James Version (KJV) – *public domain.*

Scripture quotations taken from the Amplified Bible (AMP). Copyright © 1954, 1958, 1962, 1964, 1965, 1987 by The Lockman Foundation. Used by permission. All rights reserved.

Scripture quotations taken from the Holy Bible, New International Version (NIV). Copyright © 1973, 1978, 1984, 2011 by Biblica, Inc.™. Used by permission. All rights reserved.

Scripture quotations taken from the Holy Bible, New Living Translation (NLT). Copyright ©1996, 2004, 2007 by Tyndale House Foundation. Used by permission of Tyndale House Publishers, Inc.

Paperback ISBN-13: 978-1-6628-0280-5
Hardcover ISBN-13: 978-1-6628-0281-2
eBook ISBN-13: 978-1-6628-0282-9

This book is dedicated to the Almighty God, who gave me the inspiration for writing this book.

To my beloved husband Apostle Bruce Doyle whom have taught and trained me for ministry, children Kenyon (Chinel), Shatika, grandchildren Kanye, Maia, my beloved grandmother Lottie Green (deceased), mom Mary Green, aunt Earnestine, cousin Natalie, thanks for believing and encouraging me every step of the way.

To my Kingdom family, thanks for being a source of great strength, Patricia (deceased), Hazel, Pam, Donna, Shatika, Jacoba, Crystal.

To the reader's that I haven't yet met, who maybe having a difficult time in recognizing the call of God upon their lives, trust God's timing and do not give up!

AUTHOR'S NOTE

My journey started in July of 2007, after what was supposed to be a seven-day tent revival but which lasted 21 days instead. My experience was a powerful display of God; people received salvation, healing, and deliverance. During this revival, I received so many revelations and began to write down

my thoughts in journals. At first, I thought my entries would be good for sermons until God asked me a question using this word comincia which is Italian for "to start, begin, new beginnings."

The first time I noticed this word used was "Have you started the book I lent you?"

Because of my experience of having so many setbacks and failures throughout my ministry, I believe God has anointed me to encourage those who have lost their hunger and thirst for His presence. Many of you may be at the door, at the threshold point of breakthrough in faith, and are just not realizing that the enemy is taunting you and trying to stop you from moving forward.

Remember, God's purpose isn't to abandon you, but rather, to ground you in faith. When you become discouraged, keep moving, keep pressing, keep preaching, and keep praying. Just keep on, and don't look back. Wait for God and find out what actions He wants you to take. Be still, and make sure you know which way God is leading you.

Chosen ones must go through a process.

Isaiah 43:2 (NASB) says,

> "When you pass through the waters, I will be with you, and through the rivers, they will not overflow you. When you walk through the fire, you will not be scorched, nor will the flame burn you."

Be strong, courageous, and firm. Fear not, for the Lord is redeeming His people, including all of those who were trapped or hidden in the snare of the enemy.

God is actively calling His people back into the kingdom of God. He wants to do extraordinary things through your life, and you can trust Him to guide you in ways that are trustworthy and good. Isaiah 43:18–19 (NASB) says, "Do not call to mind the former things, or ponder things of the past. Behold, I will do something new. Now it will spring forth; will you not be aware of it? I will even make a roadway in the wilderness, rivers in the desert."

It is because of the Lord's mercy and loving kindness that we are not consumed by things which come to rob our purpose and destiny. Walk humbly before the Lord during this new decade.

"Commit your works to the Lord, and your plans will be established" (Prov. 16:3 NASB). Heed His divine call, even when you don't fully understand it. Keep pressing toward the goal, and forget what lies behind you.

God will interrupt your life with overwhelming circumstances to move you in His perfect will. Let Him use you, whether in good or hard times. Stay focused; keep your eyes on the Lord. When you hold onto hope, it is the anchor of your soul. Do not allow anything or anyone to pull you out of this season of restoration.

TABLE OF CONTENTS

PART I: The Call (Trial)

1. The Process 1
2. Many Are Called, but Few Are Chosen. 13
3. Reevaluate, Realign, Refocus 24
4. Refocusing Your Priorities 37
5. Sound Your Alarm 43
6. The Discipline of Kingdom Mentality. 51
7. Unleash the Hidden Potential Inside of You 65

PART II: The Mandate (Proving)

8. Transition Into Your New Season 79
9. Igniting the Fire of Evangelism 87
10. Our Kingdom Authority 98
11. The Hidden Warriors of God 105
12. Revisiting Your Spiritual Foundation 120

PART III: The Assignment (Approval)

13. Spiritual Awakening. 133
14. God's Gift Unto the Church 144
15. Spiritual Warfare. 153
16. The Ministry of the Intercessor 161
17. The Ministry of a Watchman 166
18. Travailing Prayer 170
19. Expect the Unexpected Blessings of the Lord 176
20. A Change Is Going to Come 182

PART I

The Call
(Trial)

"Commit your works to the Lord
and your plans will be established".
(Prov. 16:3 NASB)

CHAPTER 1

THE PROCESS

W hen God gives you an assignment that's bigger than you, the process becomes challenging, but you must wait and endure the process, so you do not abort the assignment. There is a three-year process to the call, a seven-year mandate, and a ten-year assignment to God's divine order. They will run concurrently of each other, for a total of thirteen years. The word process is defined as a systematic series of actions carried out to achieve a particular result.

Strong's Greek meaning of "process" is trial, proving, and approval. The process is designed to cause you to trust God in everything. Romans 8:28 (KJV) says: "And we know that all things work together for good to them that love God, to them who are the called according to his purpose."

Here are three reasons why you must wait and endure:

1. **The call** (trial) will position you to leave what seems familiar

2. **The mandate** (proving) will cause you to stand still and recognize God is with you and

3. **The assignment** (approval) will cause you to see God through the Word He speaks to you.

Psalm 62:5–6 (NASB) tells us: "My soul, wait in silence for God only, for my hope is from Him. He is my rock and my salvation, my stronghold; I shall not be shaken."

My soul (life, existence, thought, feelings, and action), wait in silence for God only. He will become your strength while you wait. The word wait literally means to have full submission, confidence, trust, and assurance in the assignment the Lord has given you. Waiting is surrendering your will and conforming to His will while you get into position to fulfill your call.

No matter what, believe in God, for He cannot deny His Word. Numbers 23:19 (NASB) says, "God is not a man, that He should lie; nor a son of man, that He should repent. Has He said, and will He not do it? Or has He spoken, and will He not make it good?"

The will of God is no mystery. It is not something you would have to wonder about; it is clearly revealed throughout the Bible. God wants you to understand His will. Those who are fully matured in Christ are able to do His will consistently. We must have a teachable spirit in order to submit to God's will. "Teach me Thy way, O LORD. I will walk in Thy truth; unite my heart to fear Thy name" (Ps. 86:11 NASB).

The Lord knows the plan (purpose) He has for you. He holds the blueprints for your divine destiny. He has predetermined what will happen concerning you. Nothing happens by chance; God has an ultimate plan for your life.

"Teach me" is an appeal for instructions. The will of God begins with us lying at the feet of Jesus on the "threshing floor," the place where God intervenes, to break you, uncovering the treasure inside of you. The word thresh means to separate grains or seeds from the chaff to which it is attached. This is where He gives instructions concerning your purpose.

We must commit our rights and control to God with every issue we encounter. Ask God for wisdom and guidance in everything you do because in your waiting process, you will be required to remove something that represents the old you. You will be required to rearrange your priorities, so your primary motivation is to glorify God. Saturate yourself with the Word of God.

This is the place where your foundations will be tested and where God will become your divine Protector. He will fight for you while you keep silent. You won't have to lift a finger in your defense. "He that dwelleth in the secret place of the most High shall abide under the shadow of the Almighty" (Ps. 91:1 KJV).

The Process

First, the call or trial is being invited or appointed to God's purpose. The call usually comes through the formula of the

Word, prayer, or circumstances. It is where you position yourself to receive the instructions of the Lord. Ezekiel 2:1–7 (NLT) instructs us:

> "Stand up, son of man, said the voice. "I want to speak with you." The Spirit came into me as he spoke, and he set me on my feet. I listened carefully to his words. "Son of man," he said, "I am sending you to the nation of Israel, a rebellious nation that has rebelled against me. They and their ancestors have been rebelling against me to this very day. They are a stubborn and hard-hearted people. But I am sending you to say to them. This is what the Sovereign Lord says!' And whether they listen or refuse to listen—for remember, they are rebels—at least they will know they have had a prophet among them. Son of man, do not fear them or their words. Don't be afraid, even though their threats surround you like nettles and briers and stinging scorpions. Do not be dismayed by their dark scowls, even though they are rebels. You must give them my messages whether they listen or not. But they won't listen, for they are completely rebellious!"

God has called us to minister to the discouraged and disgruntled people who are bitter because of their rebellion against the things of God. The call usually takes about three years to learn the instructions of the Lord; it's a divine assignment. These three years will not be wasted, but are a time of preparation, so when given the opportunity, you would have something to say about the things God has revealed to you. Not only did God call you with His purpose, but He empowered and equipped you. He has given you power and authority to proclaim the kingdom of God.

After Paul's conversion, he disappeared for about three years (Gal. 1:18 NASB "Then three years later I went up to Jerusalem to become acquainted with Cephas, and stayed with him fifteen days"). God's purpose for calling him was extraordinary and divine. He was to preach the Gospel to the heathen. In Galatians 2:7 (NLT), Paul tells us: "They saw that God had given me the responsibility of preaching the Good News to the Gentiles, just as He had given Peter the responsibility of preaching to the Jews."

One important lesson to learn from Paul is that God called him, "to reveal His Son in me, that I might preach Him among the Gentiles, I did not immediately consult with flesh and blood" (Gal. 1:16 NASB). Why, because when God calls you, everyone doesn't need to know about it immediately. You don't need to find someone to ordain you right away. Wait on the divine instructions of the Lord. Spend intimate, valuable, and quiet time with Him. Listen carefully to His instructions concerning you.

In this trial season, some people may not understand your calling because your wilderness season is a time of discovery and preparation. In time, all will be made clear about what He has called you to do. You must treasure and protect your assignment. Don't rush the process. It takes faith to trust God for the direction in your life. In Galatians 1:17 (NASB), " Nor did I go up to Jerusalem to those who were apostles before me; but I went away to Arabia, and returned once more to Damascus." The main point that Paul is making in this passage of scripture is that nobody told him the Gospel. God revealed the Gospel to him. He revealed it to Paul's heart.

Second, the Mandate—Proving an official order gives you the grace to function in a capacity with a specific mission, legal document, or commission to take over the dominion in a territory. During this time, we learn about God's timing and season, strategic prayer, restoration of the apostolic ministry, spiritual warfare, God's gift to the church, and living the spiritual life.

Jeremiah 1:9–10 (KJV) says, "Then the Lord put forth His hand and touched my mouth, and the Lord said to me: "Behold, I have put My words in your mouth. See, I have this day set you over the nations and over the kingdoms, To root out and to pull down, To destroy and to throw down, To build and to plant."

1. **Pull down**—"For the weapons of our warfare are not carnal, but mighty through God to the pulling down of strongholds" (2 Cor. 10:4 KJV).
2. **Root out**—"And the one on whom seed was sown among the thorns, this is the man who hears the word, and the worry of the world, and the deceitfulness of riches choke the word, and it becomes unfruitful" (Matt. 13:22 NASB).
3. **Throw down**—"You shall utterly destroy all the places where the nations whom you shall dispossess serve their

gods, on the high mountains and on the hills and under every green tree. And you shall tear down their altars and smash their sacred pillars and burn their Asherim with fire, and you shall cut down the engraved images of their gods, and you shall obliterate their name from that place" (Deut. 12:2-3 NASB).

4. **To build**—"But their minds were hardened; for until this very day at the reading of the old covenant the same veil remains uplifted, because it is removed in Christ " (2 Cor. 3:14 NASB).

5. **To Plant**—"Those that be planted in the house of the LORD shall flourish in the courts of our God" (Ps. 92:13 KJV).

Third is the Assignment or Approval—the task or piece of work assigned to someone. "For whatever was written in earlier times was written for our instruction, that through perseverance and the encouragement of the Scriptures we might have hope" (Rom.15:4 NASB).

You will walk through seven years of famine—a season of spiritual drought, heartache, and disappointment. It will be a season of no fresh revelations or fresh outpouring of the Holy Spirit. It's a season where everything and everyone you thought were with you walks away. It will cause a widespread scarcity of family, friends, and lack of resources.

God has set us up in the earth realm to strategically advance the kingdom of God here on earth. Psalm 24:1 (AMP) declares, "The earth is the Lord's, and the fullness of it, the world and they who dwell in it." As a five-fold ministry, we are the governmental hand of God to administer and strategically reclaim territory from Satan that belongs to the Lord by His command and mandate.

The next aspect that needs to be considered is how to operate in God's divine appointment of time and season. Psalm 32:8 (NASB) tells us: "I will instruct you and teach you in the way which you should go; I will counsel you with My eye upon you." We must learn how to discern times and seasons to effectively impact our region.

An understanding of God's time and season will help you fit into God's agenda and recognize how the blessings you have long awaited for were hidden for an appointed time. Luke 8:17 (NASB) tells us, "For nothing is hidden that shall not become evident, nor anything secret that shall not be known and come to light."

God has revealed all of His appointed seasons in Leviticus 23, in which introduces us to the seven annual feasts that Israel cele-brated. Leviticus 23:1-2 (NASB) "The Lord spoke again to Moses, saying, 'Speak to the sons of Israel, and say to them, The Lord's appointed times which you shall proclaim as holy convocations— My appointed times are these:' Passover—Leviticus 23:5 (NASB) "In the first month, on the fourteenth day of the month at twi-light is the Lord's Passover;" Unleavened Bread—Leviticus 23:6 (NASB) "Then on the fifteenth day of the same month there is the Feast of Unleavened Bread to the Lord; for seven days you shall eat unleavened bread;" The First Fruits—Leviticus 23:10 (NASB) "Speak to the sons of Israel, and say to them, 'When you enter the land which I am going to give to you and reap its harvest, then you shall bring in the sheaf of the first fruits of your harvest to the priest;" Pentecost—Leviticus 23:16 (NASB) "You shall count fifty days to the day after the seventh sabbath; then you shall present a new grain offering to the Lord;" Festival of Trumpets—Leviticus 23:24 (NASB) "Speak to the sons of Israel, saying, In the seventh month on the first of the month, you shall have a rest, a reminder by blowing of trumpets, a holy convocation;" The Day of Atonement—Leviticus 23:27 (NASB) "On exactly the tenth day of this seventh month is the day of atonement; it shall be a holy convocation for you, and you shall humble your souls and present an offering by fire to the Lord;" The Festival of Booths—Leviticus 23:34 (NASB) "Speak to the sons of Israel, saying, On the fifteenth of this seventh month is the Feast of Booths for seven days to the Lord." These feasts are rich with symbolic and prophetic significance. As believers, we are not putting ourselves under the law but simply expressing our desire to return to the biblical roots of our faith. Colossians 2:7–9 (NLT) says,

> "Let your roots grow down into him, and let your lives be built on him. Then your faith will grow strong in the truth you were taught, and you will overflow with thankfulness. Don't let anyone capture you with empty philosophies and high-sounding nonsense that comes from human thinking and from the spiritual powers of this

world. For in Christ lives all the fullness of God in a human body."

Paul said in Romans 15:4 (NASB), "For whatever was written in earlier times was written for our instruction, that through perseverance and the encouragement of the Scriptures we might have hope." By celebrating Jesus in the feasts, we can learn more fully what Jesus has done for us and how to walk with Him in our everyday lives. The set feasts of the Lord give us greater insights into God's prophetic seasons. The Hebrew word feast means "appointed times." Matthew 5:17–19 (NASB) instructs us:

> "Do not think that I came to abolish the Law or the Prophets; I did not come to abolish but to fulfill. For truly I say to you, until heaven and earth pass away, not the smallest letter or stroke shall pass from the Law until all is accomplished. Whoever then annuls one of the least of these commandments, and teaches others to do the same, shall be called least in the kingdom of heaven; but whoever keeps and teaches them, he shall be called great in the kingdom of heaven."

To fulfill does not mean "to do away with," it means "to accomplish." We have been taught to believed that Jesus meant that it's no longer needed. When Jesus used the words fulfill and destroy, He was telling them that He did not come to dissolve or make the Word of God invalid, by leading them astray with false teachings.

Believers have to understand God's time and season in a way that makes it practical for them to apply and celebrate in their Christian life. They know that there must be something more than church as usual, which has not brought the manifest presence of God. When we receive His truth, and experience His presence, as believers of the Lord Jesus Christ, these promises and blessings were not only for the Jewish people because Jesus has opened the way for us to celebrate these holidays.

The sons of Issachar walked in revelatory understanding borne out of an intimate knowledge of the Lord's times and seasons, as written in 1 Chronicles 12:32 (NASB) "And of the sons of Issachar, men who understood the times, with knowledge of what Israel should do, their chiefs were two hundred; and all their kinsmen were at their command." The name Issachar means "he will bring reward." The word understanding in Hebrew is bee-nah, which means "discernment, wisdom, perception, and knowledge."

A person with an Issachar anointing understands the timing of God and seek every opportunity to release the blessings of God into its correct season. Great breakthroughs come through this unique anointing. The Issachar anointing puts us in the proper timing in the plans of God. In the spiritual realm, we need to know our time and season. For example, June is the sixth month on the Gregorian calendar, but it's the third month known as Sivan on the Bible's calendar. Esther 8:9a (NASB) tells us, "So the king's scribes were called at that time in the third month (that is, the month known as Sivan)."

There is a set time and season for everything that God has if the church will arise and fulfill its destiny on the earth in this hour. The wisdom of the sons of Issachar is much needed to sustain revival.

It's important to know when God's day begins and ends. This knowledge will confuse the enemy. Genesis 1:5 (NASB) confirms this. "God called the light day, and the darkness He called night. And there was evening and there was morning, one day". If you begin praying at the first watch (6 p.m. to 9 p.m.), you will move ahead of the plans of the enemy. Lamentations 2:19 (NASB) says, "Arise, cry aloud in the night at the beginning of the night watches; pour out your heart like water before the presence of the Lord; lift up your hands to Him for the life of your little ones who are faint because of hunger at the head of every street."

CHAPTER 2

MANY ARE CALLED,
BUT FEW ARE CHOSEN

In Matthew 22:14 (NASB), Jesus said, "For many are called, but few are chosen." The King sends out an invitation three times. Each time it was rejected. God calls many, but few are chosen. Jesus shares a parable about the kingdom of heaven and how God prepared a great marriage feast for His Son and His true followers. The word called means that you are invited by God, called, and divinely selected and appointed. Chosen means appointed by God to conceive and prosper from His favor, selected or marked for favor or special privilege to produce a certain result.

When God entered the marriage feast that Jesus talks about in this parable, He immediately saw a man without the proper wedding garment of righteousness, symbolizing sincerity, repentance, humility, and obedience. This garment replaces rebellion, hypocrisy, and false profession.

The words to see mean to view attentively, to carefully look over, to closely look upon and contemplate, and inspect. The idea is that God entered the banquet feast for the purpose of looking over and inspecting the guests. He wanted to make sure everyone and everything was in order for His Son's great celebration.

There is an open invitation, but you must be responsible for wearing the proper, clean garment. God is not calling the old you, but the new you. Ephesians 4:24 (NASB) tells us to "put on the new self, which in the likeness of God, has been created in righteousness and holiness of the truth" and Ephesians 4:1 (NASB) says, "I, therefore, the prisoner of the Lord, entreat you to walk in a manner worthy of the calling with which you have been called." Philippians 1:27 (NASB) exhorts, "Only conduct yourselves in a manner worthy of the gospel of Christ, so that whether I come and see you or remain absent, I will hear of you that you are standing firm in one spirit, with one mind striving together for the faith of the gospel."

God has divinely called you with a purpose, and it only can be fulfilled by you. He wants to use your gift and passion to draw others to Him. Many people reject the call of God because it comes with a price, and not everyone is ready to pay the price. It takes years of preparation and training by the Lord and seasoned pastors. You will go through many circumstances and situations that will cause you to second-guess God.

First Peter 2:9 (NASB) informs us: "But you are a chosen race, a royal priesthood, a holy nation, a people for God's own possession, that you may proclaim the excellencies of Him who has called you out of darkness into His marvelous light."

Renew Your Mind

The Bible clearly states that the believer must undergo a radical change within their inner being in order to be used by God. Romans 12:2 (NASB) tells us: "And do not be conformed to this world, but be transformed by the renewing of your mind, that you may prove what the will of God is, that which is good and acceptable and perfect." The believer must be transformed and changed inwardly. There is a real war going on inside of you. Paul shares this with us in Romans 7:20-21 (NASB): "But if I am doing the very thing I do not wish, I am no longer the one doing it, but sin which dwells in me. I find then the principle that evil is present in me, the one who wishes to do good."

How is a believer transformed within their inner person? By the renewing of their mind. The believer's mind is to be renewed, which means to be made new, readjusted, changed, turned around, and regenerated. Because we have been affected by the sins of this world, we must test and examine ourselves to see if we are in the faith.

Because of the ongoing struggle with daily sin, the believer must keep their mind upon spiritual things and not carnal things. In Romans 8:5-7 (NASB) it says, "For those who are according to the flesh, set their minds on the things of the flesh, but those who are according to the Spirit, the things of the Spirit. For the mind set on the flesh is death, but the mind set on the Spirit is life and peace, because the mind set on the flesh is hostile toward God; for it does not subject itself to the law of God, for it is not even able to do so."

"Because the carnal mind is enmity against God; for it is not subject to the law of God, nor indeed can it be" (Rom. 8:7 NKJV). Man's mind has become blinded by Satan. Second Corinthians 4:4 (NKJV) says, "Whose minds the god of this age has blinded, who do not believe, lest the light of the gospel of the glory of Christ, who is the image of God, should shine upon them."

Man's mind has become focused upon earthly things, and this has caused their mind to become fleshly, delighting in false humility and puffed up. Titus 1:15 (NASB) tells us, "To the pure, all things are pure, but to those who are defiled and unbelieving, nothing is pure; but both their mind and their conscience are defiled."

When a person receives the Lord Jesus Christ as their Lord, they are spiritually born again and made into a new man. Having put on the new man who is renewed in knowledge, they now walk humbly in true righteousness and holiness according to the image of who created them.

Given the mind of Christ, you now have received not the spirit of the world, but the Spirit who is from God, who searches all things. The Holy Spirit comes to teach not the wisdom of man, but the spiritual things of God. "But people who aren't Christians can't understand these truths from God's Spirit. It all sounds foolish to them because only those who have the Spirit can understand what the Spirit means. We who have the Spirit understand these things, but others can't understand us at all. How could they? For, who can know what the Lord is thinking? Who can give him counsel? But we can understand these things, for we have the mind of Christ" (1 Cor. 2:14-16 NLT).

In First Corinthians 2:9–10 (NKJV), Paul encourages us, "But as it is written: 'Eye has not seen, nor ear heard, Nor have entered into the heart of man the things which God has prepared for those who love Him.'" But God has revealed them to us through His Spirit. For the Spirit searches all things, yes, the deep things of God."

The believer is to live a transformed life, which means to walk day by day, renewing his mind. In Matthew 22:37 (NKJV), "Jesus said to him, 'You shall love the Lord your God with all your heart, with all your soul, and with all your mind.'"

The Power of the Spoken Word

There are three foundational keys of faith that will get you results.

Have faith in:

(1) God (Heb. 11:1)
(2) His Word (Rom. 10:17) and
(3) His Promises (Ps. 84:11).

Faith is simply taking God at His Word. The Word of God is a true gift to mankind. God's Word is alive and powerful; when activated by faith, it produces results, miracles, salvation, healing, and answers to our prayers.

Believers are strong only as the Word of God abides in them. John 15:7 (NASB) tell us, "If you abide in Me, and My words abide in you, ask whatever you wish, and it will be done for you." The Word of God is spirit and life to those who receive it in faith. God's Word is powerful. Isaiah 55:11 (NASB) declares, "So shall My Word be which goes forth from My mouth. It shall not return to Me empty, without accomplishing what I desire, and without succeeding in the matter for which I sent it."

There is great power in the spoken word of faith that will remove obstacles, as God says in Isaiah 40:4 (NLT), "Fill in the valleys, and level the mountains and hills. Straighten the curves, and smooth out the rough places."

We must have confidence in approaching God so that He hears us when we ask for anything that pleases him. Make your request known to Him, according to His Word. We can't just say anything and everything that comes to mind and expect God to grant it. We must pray "according to His will," which is found in the Bible. His will is His Word. Combining the Word of God along with the Promises of God will activate your divine destiny.

"When Jesus came to the region of Caesarea Philippi, he asked his disciples, "Who do people say that the Son of Man is?'" "Well," they replied, "some say John the Baptist, some say Elijah, and others say Jeremiah or one of the other prophets." Then he asked them, "But who do you say I am?" Simon Peter answered, "You are the Messiah, the Son of the living God." Jesus replied, "You are blessed, Simon. son of John, because my Father in heaven has revealed this to you. You did not learn this from any human being'" (Matt. 16:13–17 NLT).

Three Keys to God's Word

We must: (1) have faith in the Father; (2) believe in the Son; and (3) obey the Holy Spirit. Pray three different scriptures each day over your circumstances and wait for the promise. There is great power and authority in the spoken Word of God. It will accomplish His purposes and desires. Isaiah 55:11 (NASB) declares: "So shall My word be which goes forth from My mouth; It shall not return to Me empty; without accomplishing what I desire, and without succeeding in the matter for which I sent it." So, when you find what God's Word says about your situation, speak it by faith, believing it's already done.

There is power in the tongue because Psalm 45:1 (NASB) says: "My heart overflows with a good theme; I address my verses to the King; My tongue is the pen of a ready writer." Let your heart be filled with the truth of God's Word. Because your words indicate what is in your heart. Proverbs 4:23 (NASB) tells us: "Watch over your heart with all diligence, for from it flow the springs of life." Words have the power to build or destroy. Jesus says in Matthew 12:35 (NASB): "The good man out of his good treasure brings forth what is good; and the evil man out of his evil treasure brings forth what is evil."

Hide the Word of God in your heart. Psalm 119:11 (KJV) admonishes us: "Thy word I have treasured in my heart, that I may not sin against Thee." God's Word is a radiant light, which guides us on the right path. Psalm 119:105 (KJV) says: "Thy word is a lamp unto my feet, and a light unto my path." The Word of God is like a hammer that scatters rock. It will remove and destroy strongholds. Meditate on it day and night.

A stronghold is a fortified place where a mindset is developed. A stronghold is an area in which a particular belief of anything one heard or held onto for years. Our minds are exposed daily, with thoughts of failure, hopeless, loneliness, and lack of resources. We must fight back these negative thoughts with the Word of God. Second Corinthians 10:4-5 (NLT) says, "We use God's mighty weapons, not worldly weapons, to knock down the strongholds of human reasoning and to destroy false arguments. We destroy every proud obstacle that keeps people from knowing God. We capture their rebellious thoughts and teach them to obey Christ."

Strongholds includes mindset. Psalm 9:9-10 (NASB) encourages us: "The Lord also will be a stronghold for the oppressed, a stronghold in times of trouble, and those who know Thy name will put their trust in Thee; for thou, O Lord, hast not forsaken those who seek Thee."

A stronghold is also a "hiding place." First Corinthians 10:13 (NASB) tells us: "No temptation has overtaken you but such as is common to man; and God is faithful, who will not allow you to be tempted beyond what you are able, but with the temptation will provide the way of escape also, that you may be able to endure it."

Strongholds are ruled by authoritative principalities. "For we do not wrestle against flesh and blood, but against principalities, against powers, against the rulers of the darkness of this age, against spiritual hosts of wickedness in the heavenly places" (Eph. 6:12 NKJV).

The mind is the territory that the enemy seeks to control because it will cause you to refuse the knowledge of truth, to refuse to glorify God, and to practice unrighteousness—which is contrary to God. Second Corinthians 4:4 (NLT) tells us, "Satan, who is the god of this world, has blinded the minds of those who don't believe. They are unable to see the glorious light of the Good News. They don't understand this message about the glory of Christ, who is the exact likeness of God."

A relationship with Jesus Christ liberates us from Satan's power. Satan works through lust to keep his captives. Lust means desire, craving, and longing, the desire for what is forbidden. These are three areas Satan uses these three areas to enslave, tempt, and control us listed in 1 John 2:16 (NASB): "For all that is in the world, the lust of the flesh, and the lust of the eyes, and the boastful pride of life, is not from the Father, but is from the world." But if you are in Christ you are freed from the bondage of sin. "It was for freedom that Christ set us free; therefore keep standing firm and do not be subject again to a yoke of slavery" (Gal. 5:1 NASB).

We should use God's mighty weapons of armor to overcome and breakthrough Satan's barrier. Ephesians 6:11 NLT says, "Put on all of God's armor so that you will be able to stand firm against all strategies and tricks of the devil."

Unshakable Faith

Unshakable faith simply means nothing can move you. No trials or crisis are able to weaken or destroy you. Because your belief system is strong. Psalm 55:22 (NASB) encourages us: "Cast your burden upon the Lord, and He will sustain you; He will never allow the righteous to be shaken." Unshakable faith means faith that is firm determination, unwavering, steadfast, unbendable, and incapable of being shaken.

Unshakable faith will shake our foundation, challenging us to pursue the things of God. Hebrews 12:28-29 (NASB) tells us: "Therefore, since we receive a kingdom which cannot be shaken, let us show gratitude, by which we may offer to God an acceptable service with reverence and awe; for our God is a consuming fire."

Have you ever experienced a season where your faith was shaken? Luke 22:31-32 (NASB) tells us: "Simon, Simon, behold, Satan has demanded permission to sift you like wheat; but I have prayed for you, that your faith may not fail; and you, when once you have turned again, strengthen your brothers."

Trials, temptations, and crisis comes to test our faith. James 1:3-4 (NASB) reminds us, "Knowing that the testing of your faith produces endurance. And let endurance have its perfect result, that you may be perfect and complete, lacking in nothing."

God will allow trials to come, to strengthen our faith. We must stand firm and let nothing move you. James 1:12 (NASB) encourages us: "Blessed is a man who perseveres under trial; for once he has been approved, he will receive the crown of life, which the Lord has promised to those who love Him." This foundation is firm because it has been and tried and tested with the approval of God. This is a sure foundation to build upon.

CHAPTER 3

REEVALUATE, REALIGN, REFOCUS

R eevaluate—consider or examine something again in order to make changes. Renew one's assessment; determine the significance, value, worth, quality of your kingdom assignment.

Realign—is where we align ourselves with the sovereign plan and purpose of God.

Refocus—the spiritual discovery process that brings renewed passion back for Christ.

These tasks are critical for us in advancing the kingdom of God. Why? Because many have fallen asleep spiritually. It's the process through which the heart grows cold to the things of God and the spiritual senses have become dull.

We have entered one of the greatest seasons of our lives when we can expect the unexpected blessings of the Lord. But if we don't shift our mindset and focus, we will not only miss our season, but the promises of the Lord. We are coming out of the shadows. Enlarge your tent. Expand your plans because you stood in faith. Go to your next place in God. Lengthen your cords, strengthen your stakes, for you will spread out to the right and to the left.

You will not be ashamed (Isa 54:2-4 NASB "Enlarge the place of your tent; stretch out the curtains of your dwellings, spare not; lengthen your cords, and strengthen your pegs. For you will spread abroad to the right and to the left. And your descendants will possess nations, and they will resettle the desolate cities. Fear not, for you will not be put to shame; neither feel humiliated, for you will not be disgraced; but you will forget the shame of your youth, and the reproach of your widowhood you will remember no more.")

God has a bigger purpose. God wants to expand your influence for His purposes. The measure of your faith is not what you can consume, but what you allow God to birth through you. It's not based on our ability, but our expandability.

> "Shout for joy, O barren one, you who have borne no child; break forth into joyful shouting and cry aloud, you who have not travailed; for the sons of the desolate one will be more numerous than the sons of the married woman," says the Lord. "Enlarge the place of your tent; stretch out the curtains of your dwellings, spare not; lengthen your cords, and strengthen your pegs. "For you will spread abroad to the right and to the left. And

your descendants will possess nations, and will
resettle the desolate cities. Fear not, for you will
not be put to shame; and do not feel humiliated,
for you will not be disgraced. But you will forget
the shame of your youth, and [with] the reproach
of your widowhood you will remember no more"
(Isa. 54:1–4 NASB).

Expand your view. Ephesians 3:20 (NASB) states, "Now to Him
who is able to do exceeding abundantly beyond all that we ask or
think, according to the power that works within us."

It's time to break forth and travail in your region. In Matthew
23:37-39 (NASB) Jesus says: "O Jerusalem, Jerusalem, who kills
the prophets and stones those who are sent to her! How often I
wanted to gather your children together, the way a hen gathers her
chicks under her wings, and you were unwilling. "Behold, your
house is being left to you desolate! "For I say to you, from now
on you shall not see Me until you say, 'BLESSED IS HE WHO
COMES IN THE NAME OF THE LORD!'"

"You are the chosen Servant of the Lord. God, the
LORD, created the heavens and stretched them
out. He created the earth and everything in it. He
gives breath and life to everyone in all the world.
And it is he who says, I, the LORD, have called you
to demonstrate my righteousness. I will guard and
support you, for I have given you to my people as
personal confirmation of my covenant with them.

And you will be a light to guide all nations to me. You will open the eyes of the blind and free the captives from prison. You will release those who sit in dark dungeons" (Isa. 42:5-7 NLT). It's all for His glory!

In Ezekiel 36:27 (NLT) it says, "And I will put my Spirit in you so you will obey my laws and do whatever I command," which means that God has qualified you for this work and office. God will bring forth revival. True revival brings forth the recovery of biblical truth. It's not a matter of emotions but the heart of genuine repentance that will cause people to come under deep conviction.

Take the limits off of God. God is able to fulfill all promises, even if they seem humanly impossible. Romans 4:21 (NASB) says, "And being fully assured that what God had promised, He was able also to perform." God's Word is the surest thing. He is able, and He is faithful, but you must be fully persuaded of this. God is able to make grace abound, God is able to give you much more, and God is able to subdue all things. Our expectations limit what we receive from the Lord. What God is doing is immeasurable (which means incapable of being measured, limitless, too great to be measured). It is supernatural, going beyond all measure.

Ephesians 3:19–20 (NASB) encourages us "to know the love of Christ which surpasses knowledge, that you may be filled up to all the fullness of God. Now to Him who is able to do far more abundantly beyond all that we ask or think, according to the power that works within us."

Exceeding—to surpass; to go beyond any request; to overcome and do anything.

Abundantly—to overflow and to do more than enough

Above—to go over and above, beyond any need

In these verses, Paul announces his confidence in the power of God to both hear and answer prayer. The idea here is to demand something that is due to you because of your redemptive rights. If we change our thinking, God can change our circumstances. He loves to show His exceedingly abundantly power in hopeless, impossible situations. Why? Because He is El Shaddai, God Almighty.

Change Your Destiny

Your destiny is a matter of choice. Who we are consist of our thoughts and beliefs, because life is filled with storm and difficulties. But you have the power to change your destiny by the words you speak. Isaiah 50:4 (KJV) tells: "The Lord GOD hath given me the tongue of the learned, that I should know how to speak a word in season to him that is weary: he wakeneth this morning by morning, he wakeneth mine ear to hear as the learned."

One prophetic word from the Lord could shift your destiny. But if you are not careful, doubt and unbelief will cancel the blessings of the Lord in your due season. Proverbs 15:23 (NASB) inspires us: "A man has joy in an apt answer, and how delightful is a timely word!"

2 Kings 7:1-3 (NASB) tells us about a king's royal officer, who missed out from receiving his blessings, because of doubt and unbelief: "Then Elisha said, "Listen to the word of the Lord; thus says the Lord, "Tomorrow about this time a measure of fine flour shall be sold for a shekel, and two measures of barley for a shekel, in the gate of Samaria."" And the royal officer on whose hand the king was leaning answered the man of God and said, "Behold, if the LORD should make windows in heaven, could this thing be?" Then he said, "Behold you shall see it with your own eyes, but you shall not eat of it." Now there were four leprous men at the entrance of the gate; and they said to one another, "Why do we sit here until we die?""

The prophet Elisha specified the time and price, when plenty would manifest in the city. But the king's royal officer doubted the prophecy and the power of God. Because of his unbelief, it canceled the blessings of God. But, there were four leprous men who remain at the gate, with absolutely nothing to lose. They had two options: stay there and starve to death, or go out to the camp of the Arameans and surrender to them. When you have exhausted all possibilities, that's the place where God performs miracles. So, as the lepers approach the enemy camp, the last thing they expected to find was a underserved miracle. When we receive and obey the prophetic Word of the Lord, things can change quickly. God's Word is sure. Ezekiel 12:25–28 (NASB) says,

"For I the Lord shall speak, and whatever word I speak will be performed. It will no longer be delayed, for in your days, O rebellious house, I shall speak the word and perform it, declares the Lord God. Furthermore, the word of the Lord came to me, saying, "Son of man, behold, the house of Israel is saying, 'The vision that he sees is for many years from now, and he prophesies of times far off.' Therefore say to them, "Thus, says the Lord God, "None of My words will be delayed any longer. Whatever word I speak will be performed," declares the Lord God.""

Enter into God's kingdom of power and "do not be seized with alarm and struck with fear, little flock, for it is your Father's good pleasure to give you the kingdom" (Lk. 12:32 AMP). Matthew 5:14 (NASB) tells us: "You are the light of the world. A city set on a hill cannot be hidden." Believing together in unity can dispel the spiritual darkness wherever we live, work, and travel. If the light of God within us becomes dim, we will show a weak spiritual light, and God's kingdom will not advance in our lives or cities.

As a spirit-filled, born again believer, the kingdom of God flows in and through us like a river of living water. The word flows means movement, a stream, unhindered and not stationary. In John 4:13-14 (NASB), Jesus says: "Everyone who drinks of this water shall thirst again; but whoever drinks of the water that I shall give him shall never thirst; but the water that I shall give him shall become in him a well of water springing up to eternal life."

God governs and rules over everything according to Psalm 103:19 (NASB): "The LORD has established His throne in the heavens; and His sovereignty rules over all." He rules over territory, sickness, poverty, and demonic forces." The earth is the Lord's and the fullness of it, the world and they who dwell in it" (Ps. 24:1 AMP). Because we are a part of His kingdom, He has given us authority to rule. Luke 10:19 (NASB) assures us: "Behold, I have given you authority to tread on serpents and scorpions, and over all the power of the enemy, and nothing will injure you." "The earth is the Lord's, and the fullness of it, the world and they who dwell in it" (Ps. 24:1 AMP).

Have you had an encounter or experience with God? Luke 17:20-21 (NASB) lets us know that "Now having been questioned by the Pharisees as to when the kingdom of God was coming, He answered them and said, 'The kingdom of God is not coming with signs to be observed; nor will they will say, 'Look, here it is!' or, 'There it is!' For behold, the kingdom of God is in your midst'".

The word experience is defined as a practical contact with and observation of facts or events. Practical knowledge of something or someone. An example of experience: (Matthew 14:19 NASB "And ordering the multitudes to recline on the grass, He took the five loaves and the two fish, and looking up toward heaven, He blessed the food, and breaking the loaves He gave them to the disciples, and the disciples gave to the multitudes"). Jesus fed the multitude with human supplies so they had the practical knowledge of who He was.

The word encounter is defined as having to meet with unexpectedly, a direct meeting. An encounter example: John 4:7-10 NASB "There came a woman of Samaria to draw water. Jesus said to her, "Give Me a drink." For His disciples had gone away into the city to buy food. The Samaritan woman therefore said to Him, "How is it that You, being a Jew, ask me for a drink since I am a Samaritan woman?" (For Jews have no dealings with Samaritans). Jesus answered and said to her, "If you knew the gift of God, and who it is who says to you, 'Give Me a drink,' you would have asked Him, and He would have given you living water."" He offered the woman at the well living waters that satisfied the inner thirst of someone who met Jesus directly, expecting nothing. Sometimes, in order to move us in the right direction, God has to interrupt our lives with an overwhelming sense of His presence. Those who worship Him must do so in Spirit and in Truth. Worship comes from within. Those who experience Him by observing only the miracles have lost their opportunity in knowing the true gift God has given them.

Persistent Faith Produces Restitution

One word can make a difference in our breakthrough. Persistent faith is the source to tap into the strength of God. In spite of obstacles, opposition, and discouragement, we must trust and have confidence in God and His ability to give us what we are praying for. Jesus says in Luke 18:1 (KJV), "Men ought always to pray, and not to faint" (which means, do not lose heart). Do not give into doubt, fear, unbelief, and discouragement, or use excuse for your unbelief in your prayers. Rebuke and resist all opposition.

We are God's chosen people. The devil has to release what belongs to us. If a godless judge can respond to constant pressure, how much more will an awesome, powerful, loving God will respond. Persistent prayer is what the Lord uses to test our character, faith, and hope until the time came to fulfill His word. One word can make a difference in our breakthrough.

Restitution versus Restoration

Restitution is shown in 2 Kings 8:6 (NLT): "Is this true? the King asked her. And she told him that it was. So, he directed one of his officials to see to it that everything she had lost was restored to her, including the value of any crops that had been harvested during her absence."

The word restitution is defined as the act of returning something that was lost or stolen to its owner; payment that is made to someone for damage or trouble. It amends damage and compensates for the actual damages. The word restoration is defined as an act of restoring or the condition of being restored; bringing back to a former position or condition, to fix or repair.

Instead of asking God to fix or repair something, we need to be asking God to amend and compensate us for the actual damage of something that actually belongs to us but was stolen from us in the last season of seven years. Chosen people of God must go through a season of frustration.

The test of frustration is a season of disappointment, defeat, failure to accomplish goals, and a tough life. Everyone who tries to accomplish something experiences frustrations. It is only those who don't bother to try to accomplish anything who don't experience frustration. It is a normal process of those who are trying to do something. The more effort you invest into trying to accomplish or achieve something, the more frustration you will experience. Frustration is to bring to nothing, to break, to nullify, to make void, and to disappoint. It's an emotion that occurs in situations where one is blocked from reaching a personal goal. It will occur whenever your actions are producing fewer results than you think they should. Sometimes, God allows our plan to be frustrated because it's simply not His time or His will.

Restitution means giving back; the return of something to its rightful owner. Restoration means the return of something to the condition it was in before it was changed. The widow didn't lose her home or land; she surrendered it upon the Word of God released by the prophet Elisha.

God Seekers Will Release the Fire of Revival

When Asa became king in 2 Chronicles 14:1 (NASB) the land was undisturbed for ten years, he faced his first major test, and it was this test that lit the fire. He encouraged his people to seek the Lord and led them to build and prosper. You can't seek the Lord with a divided heart. Obedience to God will give you peace with Him and others. Whatever idol you set before Him will cause you to lose your connection with God.

Deuteronomy 4:29 (NLT) says, "From there you will search again for the Lord your God. And if you search for him with all your heart and soul, you will find him." The power of one person seeking God with all their heart can cause a revival to break out. King Asa confessed his own weakness, and then he acknowledged the limitless power of God. He realized that this battle belonged to the Lord and called upon Him to defend His honor. "Then Asa called to the Lord his God and said, Lord, there is no one besides Thee to help in the battle between the powerful and those who have no strength; so help us, O Lord our God, for we trust in Thee, and in Thy name have come against this multitude. O Lord, Thou art our God; let not man prevail against Thee. So, the Lord routed the Ethiopians before Asa and before Judah, and the Ethiopians fled" (2 Chron. 14:11-12 NASB).

As a seeker of the Lord, you must be planted like a tree on the side of a river, withstanding every wind and storm of life. "And he shall be like a tree planted by the rivers of water, that bringeth forth his fruit in his seasons, his leaf also shall not wither; and whatsoever he doeth shall prosper" (Ps 1:3 KJV). Revival never comes through the power of human strength, but through faith and the power of God. We must be fully committed to God's limitless power.

Have you ever noticed a person whose car wouldn't start until they got somebody to help them push it or let it roll until it got started? Then, one day that person ran into someone who knew a little more about cars, who popped the hood and said, "I think this is your problem," and he reached down, connected a loose wire, and the car started right up.

The power was there the whole time, but a loose connection was the problem. Now, how does that apply to our lives? When our connection is loose and apart from God, we have limited power. It will be hard to jump the fire of the Holy Spirit, which produces a revival.

Revival comes to rekindle the fire of passion for Christ in your spirit. When a person has been dragged in life because of circumstances and disappointment, the flame of fire seems to go dim. And they begin to ponder on whether God still hears their prayers or not, needing to refocus their priorities.

CHAPTER 4

REFOCUSING YOUR PRIORITIES

H aggai issues a clear call to his own people and to us that we should set ourselves to the task assigned to us by God. We should not allow difficulties, enemies, or selfish pursuits turn us away from our divinely given responsibilities. We need the cooperation of everyone to demonstrate the necessity for teamwork in carrying out God's purposes on Earth. Consider your ways, consider what you have done to neglect God's house. The people were using their poverty, food shortages, and inflation as excuses not to finish the temple.

Don't underestimate your capacity for change. There is never a right time to do a difficult thing. Some of our priorities are out of focus because we are afraid of what God might ask us to do in rearranging our priorities. We fear that a change in our priorities may cause conflict in our life, causing us to do without the things we really enjoy.

God wants to do extraordinary things through your life, and you can trust Him to guide you in ways that are trustworthy and good. Haggai 1:4 is diagnosing misplaced priorities, "Is it time for you yourselves to dwell in your paneled houses while this house lies desolate?" True priorities are revealed in how we spend our time and money. The people in Jerusalem thought that their priorities were just fine. They started out strong, but something happened, and they lost their focus. They were faced with economic struggle and political instability, so to put off rebuilding the temple probably made sense from a human perspective. Yet, God knew that the real problem wasn't the economy; the real problem was misplaced priorities among God's people.

Your Seed Has a Divine Assignment

God spoke this word to me, explaining the "assignment of the seed." He said before we were conceived, He had already given our seed an assignment. God said in Jeremiah 1:5 (NASB): "Before I formed you in the womb I knew you, and before you were born I consecrated you; I have appointed you a prophet to the nations."

Five predictions came to Jeremiah in the first ten verses of chapter 1:

1. "But the Lord said unto me, say not, I am a child: for thou shalt go to all that I shall send thee." Within you I have planted a seed that must produce a harvest in their season. This is your season! God is saying to us, stop giving me excuses why we can't go where

He has commanded us. Your seed has an assignment. This is a divine assignment that could save and deliver someone's life.

2. "Whatsoever I command, you will speak." You must obey My command. The seed you are carrying has my plan with a kingdom assignment within it. I know the heart of My people. Speak what the Holy Spirit commands you. Not your will, but My will shall be done. You must grow and mature; change your ways, thoughts and attitudes; and learn to set your priorities with Mine. If you follow My plans, there is a key which opens up life, a key to all the mysteries of life, which enables us to stand in the face of adversity and to be stable and strong no matter what our circumstances are.

3. "I will deliver you." God says, "He did not give us the spirit of fear, but of power, love, and of a sound mind" (2 Tim. 1:7 KJV). Stop wavering in your thoughts and actions. Be stable in your walk.

4. "I have put My word in your mouth." Don't rely on your spirit, but trust in the Holy Spirit. I need you to use your delegated authority to declare and decree My words in the atmosphere on Earth. Speak My Word, and My Word will go out and accomplish what I have sent it to do. When you speak it, healing, miracles, and deliverance will take place in your family, community, church, state, and country.

5. "I have this day set you over the nations and over kingdoms, to root out, pull down, destroy, throw down, build, and plant." God says, on this day, prayers will be answered, victory will be gained,

joy will be restored, healing will take place, and every type of addiction will be broken because He has equipped us, no matter how inadequate you may feel. His call is not based on a person's ability to think, their appearance, or their voice quality. God's call is based on a person's heart and on how open and dedicated it will be. A surrendered heart is what God wants.

The seed God has planted in us must grow, flourish, and produce a harvest of soul. He planted seeds of His kindness and character. Our assignment has never been to conform to what the world is doing. God gives us free will. He wants us to choose between what's right or wrong.

When God released the seed, we become an ambassador for heaven. When God told Moses to send out the spies to search the land of Canaan (Num. 13), the Lord said to Moses, "Send men to explore the land of Canaan, the land I am giving to Israel." So, Moses gave the men these instructions as he sent them out to explore the land. "Go northward through the Negev into the hill country. See what the land is like and find out whether the people living there are strong or weak, few or many" (Num. 13:17-18 NLT). We serve a God who is omnipotent (all powerful), omniscient (all knowing), and omnipresent (being everywhere at once).

God had already told them about the land (Deut. 1:21 NASB "See, the Lord your God has placed the land before you; go up, take possession, as the Lord, the God of your fathers, has spoken to you. Do not fear or be dismayed"), but the people did not believe God and wanted Moses to send spies to go out and search the land. If they had gone in and possessed the land, a forty-year wasted journey would have lasted probably one day. Our disobedience to God's Word could cost us to miss out on the many blessings He has in store for us.

Our mouth and rebellious spirit keeps us in our trial and circumstances longer than we are supposed to. The spies went to the land and got discouraged because of what they saw in the natural, not realizing that if they saw the land God had seen in the spiritual, they would have moved instantly and begun receiving the promises and blessings that were meant for them.

We miss many of our blessings because we get too caught up in the negative aspect of our circumstances and miss out on what God is trying to get us to focus on, which is His Word and His glory. Whatever you're facing now in your life is not for you to stay in longer than you have. The decision is yours. You can trust God to bring you out in His timing and reap the harvest of blessings that He has for you, or you can continue complaining, getting discouraged, miss out on the blessings, and stay in those circumstances longer than God intended for you to stay.

Some of us need to move out of our wilderness experience into the land flowing with milk and honey. You have been in this place and state of mind long enough. A wilderness experience is a place of vulnerability, loneliness, hopelessness, or a place of uncertainty.

The language of an unbelieving saint is always, "We are not able; we are not as strong as they are." But the language of a true believer is found in 2 Corinthians 5:7 (NASB), "For we walk by faith, and not by sight." That means we don't care what it or they look like, we trust God to bring it to pass and to deliver us to a place of overflowing and abundance of joy and blessings.

God will overthrow anybody on your property or in your house illegally and let the rightful owner take what belongs to them. Don't allow your giant to stop you from receiving your harvest. Don't look at it in the natural, but in the spiritual. God has delegated authority to His seed here on earth to overthrow Satan, his horsemen, and demons off our property, homes, marriages, and finances.

Change the way you view things and begin to say to your giants, "As long as the Lord is with me, He will provide and bless us because we know the Lord is with us, and we don't fear our enemies." Don't use idle words when you are going through difficult times. Speak life to your situation. Trust God's Word and possess your land. It's yours; step out by faith.

CHAPTER 5

SOUND YOUR ALARM

⎯

S ounding the alarm was done with horns, signifying war and danger. The blowing of trumpets called the whole assembly together. In the Old Testament, when death crept into a city or a nation, they called for the wailing women because they expressed deep sorrow and tears are powerful prayers. The blowing of the trumpet produces a vibration producing sound; what is produced when something vibrates is that someone can hear it. The sound is heard when mechanisms inside the ear send electrical impulses to the brain. A sound wave is the pattern of disturbance caused by the movement of energy traveling through a medium (such as air, water, or any other liquid or solid matter) as it propagates away from the source of the sound.

The sound God wants us to make will change our atmosphere, climate, and strongholds. Our greatest challenge is making our voice heard to establish an atmosphere that's receptive to the things of God.

Scripture says, in Jeremiah 9:17-21 (NASB), "Thus says the Lord of hosts, Consider and call for the mourning women, that they may come; and send for the wailing women, that they may come! And let them make haste, and take up a wailing for us, that our eyes may shed tears, and our eyelids flow with water. For a voice of wailing is heard from Zion, how we are ruined! We are put to great shame, for we have left the land, because they have cast down our dwellings. Now hear the word of the Lord, O you women, and let your ear receive the word of His mouth; teach your daughters wailing, and everyone her neighbor a dirge. For death has come up through our windows; it has entered our palaces, to cut off the children from the streets, the young men from the town squares." Come, let us gather at the door of the Outer Courts, "Let the priests, the Lord's ministers, weep between the porch and the altar, and let them say, "Spare Thy people, O Lord, and do not make Thine inheritance a reproach, a byword among the nations. Why should they among the peoples say, 'Where is their God?" (Joel 2:17 NASB). This is a place of intercession, a place of sacrifice and not popularity.

Our culture has become accustomed to the premature death of our young men. It has dominated and influenced our attitude and behavior. Whatever spirit controls our mind also controls our thoughts and actions. It's time to sound the alarm, letting the enemy know God will give us victory in this battle.

A Time of Regathering

The Lord told Israel "Fear not" for they were the chosen ones because of the sufferings and trials they had endured. First Corinthians 1:27 (NASB) tells us: "But God has chosen the foolish things of the world to shame the wise, and God has chosen the weak things of the world to shame the things which are strong." He says, "When you pass through the waters, I will be with you; and through the rivers, they will not overflow you. When you walk through the fire, you will not be scorched, nor will the flame burn you" (Isa. 43:2 NASB).

You have been set up to be blessed, to test your attitude and see if you would remain obedient and altogether agreeable (to follow His orders) in everything. You have been spiritually adopted to endure the waters of affliction. Go deeper in His praise, in His worship, and in His Words.

God has given you a divine promise where he will release unmerited favor and grace upon you. There will be a regathering of all scattered, broken vessels of the Lord from every geographical direction, the ones He has created for His glory.

The word glory is kavod in the Hebrews. It means heaviness, weight, or worthiness. The glory of Yahweh means the revelation of God's being, nature, and presence to mankind. His divine presence is in the midst of "where two or three are gathered together in His Name, there am He is in the midst of them" (Matt. 18:20 NASB).

This is God's promise to those who are in distress, "Let not let your heart be troubled; believe in God, believe also in Me" (John 14:1 NASB).

Then He says in Isaiah 43:8 (KJV), "Bring forth the blind people that have eyes, and the deaf that have ears." Because God is the Creator who has formed thee, He wants to do a new thing in your life. The natural man can't understand spiritual things, as 1 Corinthians 2:14 (NASB) says,

> "But a natural man does not accept the things of the Spirit of God; for they are foolishness to him; and he cannot understand them, because they are spiritually appraised."

He told the children of Israel in Isaiah 43:18–19 (NASB) , "Do not call to mind the former things; or ponder things of the past. Behold, I will do something new, now it will spring forth; will you not be aware of it? I will even make a roadway in the wilderness, rivers in the desert." The word perceive means to know, recognize, acknowledge, be aware of and understand. Here the children of Israel had failed God miserably, yet God still loved them and wanted to help them change. Notice God's message of forgetting the former things. Let go of your past hurt, your past failure, and your broken dreams. Don't dwell on them.

Change your focus. Stop making up excuses and make a fresh start instead. Stop blaming other people for your failure. It was your choice. Proverbs 28:13 (AMP) says, "He who covers his transgressions will not prosper, but whoever confesses and forsakes his sins will obtain mercy." We all need a fresh start. Stop dwelling on the past. Move forward and discover what God wants for you.

You have a choice to stay in captivity by making excuses, blaming everyone else for your failures, and feeling sorry for yourself; or to move in faith and watch God do a new work, a new miracle, and give you a new victory. The choice is yours. Faith is doing the thing you fear the most. So, focus your thoughts. God has already begun to set in motion a new way, a new direction, and a new purpose for your life. Will you follow Him? "For He is our God and we are the people of His pasture and the sheep of His hand. Today, if you will hear His voice, do not harden your hearts, as in the rebellion, as in the day of trial in the wilderness" (Ps 95:7-8 NKJV).

Has Your Love for Christ Grown Deeper or Has It Lost Its Fervency?

Fervency is defined as warmth or intensity of feeling, zeal, or passion.

You have a desire to walk in righteousness, but the sinful nature opposes and reject the spiritual things of God. Paul says in Romans 7:19-21 (NASB), "For the good that I want, I do not do, but I practice the very evil that I do not want. But if I am doing the very thing I do not want, I am no longer the one doing it, but sin which dwells in me. I find then the principle that evil is present in me, the one who wants to do good."

Are you drifting away spiritually? But have a desire to walk in righteousness. Hebrews 2:1 (NASB) gives us a specific warning: "For this reason we must pay closer attention to what we have heard, lest we drift away it." Hebrews 11:1 (NASB) tells us: "Now faith is the assurance of things hoped for, the conviction of things not seen."

"Assurance of things"—being certain in the mind; a positive declaration intended to give confidence; a promise.

"Hope for"—a feeling of expectation and desire for a certain thing to happen; to desire with expectation of obtainment or fulfillment.

"Conviction of things not seen"—a strong persuasion or belief.

Faith is the spiritual foundation of the confidence, trust, and assurance of our prayer. Hebrews 10:23 (NASB) says, "Let us hold fast the confession of our hope without wavering, for He who promised is faithful."

Without faith, there is no hope or trust that God is able to help you in every obstacle or circumstances you are facing. When you recognize that you are drifting, you must repent and return to God. First John 1:9 (NASB) admonishes us: "If we confess our sins, He is faithful and righteous to forgive us our sins and to cleanse us from all unrighteousness."

Jesus is calling His disciples together to be a witness of His resurrection power and to preach the Gospel to those "who have an ear to hear what the Spirit of the Lord is saying" (Rev. 3:22 NASB). Jesus's greatest Commission is for us to, "Go therefore and make disciples of all the nations, baptizing them in the name of the Father and the Son and the Holy Spirit" (Matt. 28:19 NASB). Christ's redemptive message is to be offered by all who belong to Him.

The word commissioned is defined as to give an order for or authorize; to bring into working condition. An authoritative order, charge, or direction; to carry out a particular task or duty; given official approval to act. You must have full confidence, trust, and assurance in the assignment God has given you. First John 5:15 (NASB) states, "And if we know that He hears us in whatever we ask, we know that we have the requests which we have asked from Him."

How do we know Him? We know Him by (1) personal fellowship; (2) overcoming the world and Satan; (3) acknowledging God and Christ; and (4) doing righteousness.

Second Corinthians 5:17 (NASB) says, "Therefore, if any man is in Christ, he is a new creature; the old things have passed away; behold, new things have come."

No matter what, you must believe on the name of the Son of God. Faith is the spiritual foundational life of a prayer warrior. Praying God's will means you must ask and seek accordingly to His Word. Isaiah 65:24 (AMP) tells us, "It shall also come to pass that before they call, I will answer; and while they are still speaking, I will hear." Let the Holy Spirit teach, guide and inspire you to walk in faith, "and all things you ask for in prayer, believing, you shall receive" (Matt. 21:22 NASB).

CHAPTER 6

THE DISCIPLINE OF KINGDOM MENTALITY

This means we are under the reign of God—past, present, and future. He is in charge of all things, sovereign in heaven and in our will. Leading others is not about our ability but about His ability to allow His will to develop ours, as He is our future hope.

Submission means the action or fact of accepting one yielding to a superior force or to the will or authority of another person. Romans 8:7 (KJV) "Because the carnal mind is enmity against God; for it is not subject to the law of God, neither indeed can be." A carnal mind is pertaining to or characterized by the flesh or the body, its passions and appetites, sensual, not spiritual, merely human, temporal, and worldly.

Moral Conditions of a Carnal Mind

1. Sinful Walk (they reject the will of God)—Jeremiah 7:23–24 (NASB) "But this is what I commanded them, saying, Obey My voice, and I will be your God, and you will be My people; and you will walk in all the way which I command you, that it may be well with you. Yet they did not obey or incline their ear but walked in their own counsels and in the stubbornness of their evil heart, and went backward and not forward."

2. Spiritual Darkness (they have no relationship with God)—Ephesians 4:18 (NASB) "Being darkened in their understanding, excluded from the life of God because of the ignorance that is in them, because of the hardness of their heart."

3. Spiritual Ignorance (they have closed their ears and eyes to truth)—Isaiah 59:8 (NASB) "They do not know the way of peace, And there is no justice in their tracks; they have made their paths crooked, whoever treads on them does not know peace."

You must demolish your old mindset and put on the new mindset for ministry by having intimate fellowship with Christ and abiding in His Words, through the guidance of the Holy Spirit. A person's attitude is dictated by his mindset. He is controlled by what he believes and not by what he knows.

How Do We Win the Day-to-Day Battle?

We win by:

- Submission (yield your will to God's will);
- Faith (totally rely on God and walk in the stability of His Words by standing firm on what it says);
- Fervent Prayer (when you meet spiritual resistance, continue to pray; that resistance will build strength in your inner being as you press in, contend, resist and fight); and
- Endurance (we must be battle ready against forces that seems to undermine your strength in the Lord.)

Achieving Victory Through Totally Surrendering to God

Psalms 86:11 (NLT) says, "Teach me your ways, O LORD, that I may live according to your truth! Grant me purity of heart, so that I may honor you." A commitment to obedience is the hallmark of one who has surrendered his life to God, for surrendering means that you will look to the Scriptures for guidance. By surrendering, you become a willing vessel, allowing God to use you for service unto Himself so that He may be glorified in your life. So, surrendering to God means living a life that is in alignment with God's Word. Without totally surrendering, you will find that your own self-interest and pride will cause you to reject the gift of God. Without totally surrendering, we attempt to work for God instead of letting God work through us. Without total surrendering to Jesus, your fleshly body will always demand more.

It is not until you surrender your life fully and completely to Christ that God can bless you as much as He really wants to. Spiritual growth stops when a person begins to prevent God from exercising control in their lives, when a person takes his eyes off God, and when a person moves ahead of God and decides to do the leading. That's when the barriers against sin begin to break down and man's worldly flesh begins to take over and allow sin to enter. In Paul's letter to the church in Corinth, Paul wrote, "Therefore I am well content with weakness, with insults, with distresses, with persecutions, with difficulties, for Christ's sake; for when I am weak, then I am strong" (2 Cor. 12:10 NASB).

Paul had discovered that strength was found in weaknesses, so he decided to surrender to the Lord as he humbly walked through life's ups and downs. It came from a perspective of keeping his eyes focused on Jesus.

These are six words the Holy Spirit revealed to me that we don't hear preached too often.

1. Repentance—a change of mind or direction, a sincere turning away, in both the mind and heart. Second Corinthians 7:10 (NASB) says, "For the sorrow that is according to the will of God produces a repentance without regret, leading to salvation, but the sorrow of the world produces death.

2. Sanctification—to make holy or to purify; to be set apart for holy use. In Second Timothy 2:21 (NASB), Paul

instructs us, "Therefore, if a man cleanses himself from these things, he will be a vessel for honor, sanctified, useful to the Master, prepared for every good work."

3. Justification—declaring a person to be just or righteous. Romans 5:1 (NASB) says, "Therefore, having been justified by faith, we have peace with God through our Lord Jesus Christ."

4. Purification—to free from guilt or evil, free from everything that pollutes. John 14:6 (NASB)says, "Jesus said to him, 'I am the way, and the truth, and the life; no one comes to the Father but through Me.'"

5. Holiness—consecrated to God's service; set apart to the service or worship of God; pure in heart. First Peter 1:14-16 (NASB) tells us, "As obedient children, do not be conformed to the former lusts which were yours in your ignorance, but like the Holy One who called you, be holy yourselves also in all your behavior because it is written, 'You shall be holy, for I am holy.'"

6. Surrendering—means to yield ownership, to relinquish control over what we are to God, we are simply acknowledging that what we "own" actually belongs to Him. He is the giver of all good things. We are responsible to care for what God has given us, as stewards of His property, but by surrendering to God, we admit that He is ultimately in control of everything, including our present

circum- stances. Surrendering to God helps us to let go of whatever has been holding us back from God's best for our lives. By surrendering to God, we let go of whatever has kept us from wanting God's way first. Matthew 16:24-26 (NASB) states, "Then Jesus said to His disciples, 'If anyone wishes to come after Me, he must deny himself, and take up his cross and follow Me. For whoever wishes to save his life will lose it but whoever loses his life for My sake will find it. For what will it profit a man if he gains the whole world and forfeits his soul? Or what will a man give in exchange for his soul?'"

What Are You Waiting For?

Are you waiting for anything? What are you expecting God to do? Waiting is hard and frustrating because of it's uncertainties. Waiting on God helps us to focus on His purpose and direction. Proverbs 19:21 (NASB) teaches us: "Many are the plans in a man's heart, but the counsel of the Lord, it will stand." Waiting is a sign of humility. Through the waiting process, God shapes you into the vessel He wants to use.

In the Gospel of Luke we found two people who were waiting in anticipation for someone. Luke 2:25 (NASB) says: "And behold, there was a man in Jerusalem whose name was Simeon, and this man was just and devout waiting for the Consolation of Israel, and the Holy Spirit was upon him." Simeon means God has heard. Luke 2:36 (NASB) says: "And there was a prophetess, Ana the daughter of Phanuel, of the tribe of Asher. She was advanced in years, having lived with a husband seven years after her marriage." Anna name mean Grace.

Simeon was "waiting for the Consolation of Israel." The word consolation means comfort, help, or rescue. He was waiting on the coming Messiah and Redeemer. The One who would bring comfort, peace, relief to the people of Israel. Second Thessalonians 2:16-17 (KJV) says: "Now our Lord Jesus Christ himself, and God, even our Father, which hath loved us, and hath given us everlasting consolation and good hope through grace, comfort your hearts, and stablish you in every good word and work."

We could always count on God to fulfill His Word. Second Corinthians 1:18-20 (NASB) inspires us: "But as God is faithful, our word to you is not yes and no. For the Son of God, Christ Jesus, who was preached among you by us—by me and Silvanus and Timothy—was not yes and no, but is yes in Him. For as many as may be the promises of God, in Him they are yes; wherefore also by Him is our Amen to the glory of God through us."

Inspite of hardship, disappointment, despair, or brokenness, stay in the presence of the Lord and stay planted in His house. Psalm 92:12-15 (NASB) declares: "The righteous man will flourish like the palm tree, he will grow like a cedar in Lebanon. Planted in the house of the LORD, they will flourish in the courts of our God. They will still yield fruit in old age; they shall be full of sap and very green, to declare that the LORD is upright; He is my rock, and there is no unrighteousness in Him." God's desire for us is that we receive all that we need to be nourished, to grow, and to be fruitful. It doesn't matter how young or old you are. We all have work to do in the kingdom of God. There is a great need for godly older people to prepare this next generation, to do the work of the Lord effectively.

Anna who was a prophetess, worshipped in the temple day and night. She was looking for redemption (grace and favor). Second Corinthians 12:9-10 (NASB) tells us: "And He has said to me, 'My grace is sufficient for you, for power is perfected in weakness.' Most gladly, therefore, I will rather boast about my weaknesses, that the power of Christ may dwell in me. Therefore I am well content with weaknesses, with insults, with distresses, with persecutions, with difficulties, for Christ's sake; for when I am weak, then I am strong."

He That Hath an Ear, Let Him Hear What the Spirit Saith Unto the Churches

Christ's purpose in sending these messages to the seven churches in Revelation Chapter 2 was to empower believers to overcome the enemy. These churches represent the spiritual conditions of strength and weaknesses found in today's church:

1) The message to the church in Ephesus: "You have patiently suffered for me without quitting. But I have this complaint you. You don't love me or each other as you did at first!" (Rev. 2:3-4 NLT)

2) The message to the church in Smyrna: "I know about your suffering and your poverty—but you are rich! I know the slander of those opposing you. They say they are Jews, but they really aren't because theirs is a synagogue of Satan." (Rev. 2:9 NLT).

3) The message to the church in Pergamum: I know that you live in the city where that great throne of Satan is located, and yet you have remained loyal to me. And you refused to deny me even when Antipas, my faithful witness, was martyred among you by Satan followers. And yet I have a few complaints against you. You tolerate some among you who are like Balaam, who showed Balak how to trip up the people of Israel. He taught them to worship idols by eating food offered to idols and by committing sexual sin." (Rev. 2:13-14 NLT).

4) The message to the church in Thyatira: "I know all the things you do—your love, your faith, your service, and your patient endurance. And I can see your constant improvement in all these things. But I have this complaint against you. You are permitting that woman—that Jezebel who calls herself a prophet—to lead my servants astray. She is encouraging them to worship idols, eat food offered to idols, and commit sexual sin." (Rev. 2:19-20 NLT).

5) The message to the church in Sardis: "I know all the things you do, and that you have a reputation for being alive—but you are dead. Now wake up! Strengthen what little

remains, for even what is left is at the point of death. Your deeds are far from right in the sight of God. Go back to what you heard and believed at first; hold to it firmly and turn to me again. Unless you do, I will come upon you suddenly, as unexpected as a thief." (Rev. 3:1-3 NLT).

6) The message to the church in Philadelphia: "I know all the things you do, and I have opened a door for you that no one can shut. You have little strength, yet obeyed my word and did not deny me." (Rev. 3:8 NLT).

7) The message to the church in Laodicea: "I know all the things you do, that you are neither hot or cold. I wish you were one or the other! But since you are like lukewarm water, I will spit you out my mouth! You say, 'I am rich, I have everything I want. I don't need a thing!' And you don't realize that you are wretched and miserable and poor and blind and naked." (Rev. 3:15-17 NLT).

Jesus wanted believers to understand that He knew exactly where they were. He saw their good work, faithfulness, and patience in the face of persecution. He also saw the bad, which included their compromise, apostasy, indifference, and lukewarmness.

Open your spirit to hear what the Spirit of God is saying to you. Yield yourself fully to the leading of the Holy Spirit. Jesus wanted these churches to understand that He knew exactly where they were. How they no longer thirst and hunger for righteousness because they have left their first love, Christ. They stopped fellowshipping with Him because of the cares of this world. Are you dedicated and committed to serving Christ to the fullest? 1 Samuel 12:24 (NASB) encourages us: "Only fear the LORD and serve Him in truth with all your heart; for consider what great things He has done for you."

The Wilderness Walk

The wilderness walk is a place where we learn to walk by faith and not feelings. It is a proving and testing time, a place where God tests what's in our hearts.

Moses was speaking to the people of Israel in Deuteronomy 8:1 (NASB) "All the commandments that I am commanding you today you shall be careful to do, that you may live and multiply, and go in and possess the land which the Lord swore to give to your forefathers." He told them, "Make sure that you obey the word, because that's going to be your survival." God tested what was in their hearts to humble them and see whether they would love Him and keep His commandments so that they might take possession of the land that was good and spacious, a land flowing with milk and honey. In their wilderness experience, they lacked nothing. The forty years of wandering in the wilderness became a test to see if these people would finally get serious about God.

If you have felt like your Christian journey has been lacking direction, God is asking you today when are you going to get serious about Him? God provided bread from heaven miraculously.

Manna means "What is it?" God provided something they weren't expecting. They were used to eating fish, cucumbers, melons, leeks, onions, and garlic in Egypt (Num. 11:5 NASB "We remember the fish which we used to eat free in Egypt, the cucumbers and the melon and the leeks, and the onions, and the garlic"). Whatever the Lord has spoken, He will do, but His provision is not always given in the manner with which we expect.

Let's look at 1 Peter 4:12-13 (NASB): "Beloved, do not be surprised at the fiery ordeal among you, which comes upon you for your testing, as though some strange thing were happening to you but to the degree that you share the sufferings of Christ, keep on rejoicing, so that also at the revelation of His glory you may rejoice with exultation."

Obedience is the acknowledgment of our obligation. Psalm 116:12-14 (NASB) asks, "What shall I render to the Lord, for all His benefits toward me? I shall lift up the cup of salvation and call upon the name of the Lord. I shall pay my vows to the Lord, Oh, may it be in the presence of all His people."

To obey God's commandments, means obeying God with our heart, our will, our mind, and our body. Temptation is a test. Satan is called the temper but having the Word of God in your loins sustains you in all things. The Word is able to expose the most hidden things before God. He wants to know what's in your minds (hearts) because Proverbs 23:7 (NASB) tells us: " For as he thinks within himself, so he is. He says to you, "Eat and drink!" The heart is the center of our life, and we must carefully guard it.

Will Your Foundation Withstand the Storm?

Jesus illustrates the importance of a secure foundation in Luke 6:46-49 (NASB) "And why do you call Me, 'Lord, Lord,' and do not do what I say? Everyone who comes to Me, and hears My words, and acts upon them, I will show you whom he is like: he is like a man building a house, who dug deep and laid a foundation upon the rock; and when a flood rose, the torrent burst against that house and could not shake it, because it had been well built. But the one who has heard, and has not acted accordingly, is like a man who built a house upon the ground without any foundation; and the torrent burst against it and immediately it collapsed, and the ruin of that house was great." Every man is building something. There are the two choices:

1—You either build on a solid and deep foundation (one that withstands the storms).

2—You build on a shallow and weak foundation (one that will not).

Psalm 46:1 (KJV) says, "God is our refuge and strength, a very present help in trouble." You are either walking God's way, experiencing His transformation in your life, and knowing His strength for difficult times, or you are walking away from God and are vulnerable to storms that may come your way. Jesus reminds us that the most important and vital thing in the life of a believer is the foundation. If the foundation is wrong, then the structure will surely be destroyed.

Our foundation is critical. There is very little difference between true Christians and the false ones from outside appearances. You can and will find both in the church. The difference between them is that when a storm hits, you can't find the false ones. They stop praising the Lord, they are sad and miserable, and some even stop coming to church.

The true believer stays in the storm. Come hell or high water, they put their trust in God and not their circumstances. Storms are sometimes short in duration but are often very intense. It will test your integrity and stability and reveal your character. A true believer must be consistent in their faith and committed to the things of God. Jesus emphasized that it is not enough to call him "Lord," that is, make a profession of faith in Him without obedience. Jesus said that those who hear and heed His Word will stand firm during the storms of life. Because the purpose of God's Word is to produce spiritual growth, it will lead and guide you. "Your Word is a lamp to my feet, and a light to my path" (Ps. 119:105 Amp).

Second Timothy 3:16-17 (NASB) informs us, "All Scripture is inspired by God and profitable for teaching, for reproof, for correction, for training in righteousness so that the man of God may be adequate, equipped for every good work."

CHAPTER 7

UNLEASH THE HIDDEN POTENTIAL INSIDE OF YOU

Ephesians 3:20 (NASB) says, "Now to Him who is able to do far more abundantly beyond all that we ask or think, according to the power that works within us." Hidden potential means moving from a fixed mindset to a develop mindset of capacity for growth, and to unleash means to set loose. It implies releasing your hidden gifts, talents, and potential; coming face to face with your greatest fear.

Proverbs 3:5-6 (KJV) encourages us: "Trust in the LORD with all thine heart; and lean not unto thine own understanding. In all thy ways acknowledge him, and he shall direct thy paths." You may have experienced times when you felt that your life had no meaning. But that is something the enemy wanted you to believe because he know if you ever get a grip on who God created you to become, you would be unstoppable in reaching the goals that are in your heart.

The Lord declares in Jeremiah 29:11 (NASB), "For I know the plans that I have for you, declares the Lord, plans for welfare and not for calamity to give you a future and a hope." You must know the source of your potential. God created everything with a purpose.

Deuteronomy 14:2 (NASB) states, "For you are a holy people to the Lord your God, and the Lord has chosen you to be a people for His own possession out of all the peoples who are on the face of the earth." Our potential is limited by what we believe cannot be done. You have a unique gift with the ability to do amazing things. But the problem is often times we don't recognize what we possess.

I want you to imagine your potential and allow the promises within you to develop and become real. First Timothy 4:15 (NLT) encourages us: "Give your complete attention to these matters. Throw yourself into your tasks so that everyone will see your progress."

According to 2 Timothy 1:9 (NLT): "It is God who saved us and chose us to live a holy life. He did this not because we deserved it, but because that was his plan long before the world began—to show his love and kindness to us through Christ Jesus." God has equipped us for the call. He has blessed us for the service. He has given us the gifts to use. So, what are you waiting on? You have been given the divine ability to subdue all things and to fulfill all promises.

Our expectations limit what we receive from God. Mark 9:23 (NASB) tells us: "And Jesus said to him, 'If You can!' All things are possible to him who believes." "If You can" is not based on the power of Jesus, but on your faith. God the Creator of everything is still performing miracles today. Nothing is too difficult for Him. He can save, heal, raise the dead, and provide for our needs. Remember, we serve a God that in His eyes, the size of our circumstances doesn't really matter. Matthew 17:20 (NASB) says: "And He said to them, 'Because of the littleness of your faith; for truly I say to you, if you have faith as a mustard seed, you shall say to this mountain, 'Move from here to there,' and it shall move; and nothing shall be impossible to you.'"

We can maximize potential, by not allowing fear to prevent us from obeying God and fulfilling His purpose in our lives. Second Timothy 1:7 (KJV) says: "For God hath not given us the spirit of fear; but of power, and of love, and of a sound mind."

According to the power that works within us. God has more in store for you than you can even imagine. The power of God can achieve in us results, which others aren't bold enough to achieve or anticipate. This power is in the person of the Holy Spirit, indwelling in a believer. John 14:26 (NASB) confirms this: "But the Helper, the Holy Spirit, whom the Father will send in My name, He will teach you all things, and bring to your remembrance all that I said to you."

What hinders "the power that worketh" in us? Jesus explains it in Matthew 13:22 (NASB): "And the one on whom seed was sown among the thorns, this is the man who hears the word, and the worry of the world, and the deceitfulness of riches choke the word, and it becomes unfruitful." The more we abandon the cares of this world and the deceitfulness of riches, the more fruitful the word will become one with us.

Take the limits off. God is able to fulfill all promises even if they seem impossible to you. God's Word is the surest thing. I am fully persuaded that God will perform what He promised. He is able to give you much more. God is able to deliver you. God is able to subdue all things. The knowledge of the Word of God is good, but we possess the knowledge; applying it to our daily lives, our circumstances and situations will change.

Our expectations limit what we receive from God. What God is doing is immeasurable. It supernaturally goes beyond our capacity of reasoning and human understanding.

Exceeding—to surpass; to go beyond any request; to overcome and do anything.

Abundantly—to overflow and to do more than enough.

Above—to go over and above; beyond any need.

We are limiting God from doing those things which are exceedingly and abundantly beyond what we ask or even think. Simply stated, there are no limits to what God can do in response to the faithful.

What is the power that works within you? It is the supernatural "dunamis" power. Again, take the limits off. If we change our thinking, God can change our lives. God loves to show His exceedingly abundant power in hopeless, impossible situations. He want us to know Him as the God who is able to do anything. He is El Shaddai, God Almighty. He is the Everlasting God, the Lord, the Creator of the ends of the Earth. He does not become weary or tired, and He gives strength to the weary. Do you know Him?

Forget the Former; Embrace the New

"Do not call to mind the former things, or ponder things of the past. Behold, I will do something new, now it will spring forth; will you not be aware of it? I will even make a roadway in the wilderness, rivers in the desert" (Isa. 43:18–19 NASB).

God does not want us to carry old emotions into the new realm of His glory. Jesus was saying two things in Luke 5:36-37 (NASB). He told them a parable. "No one tears a piece from a new garment and puts it on an old garment; otherwise he will both tear the new, and the piece from the new will not match the old. And no one puts new wine into old wineskins; otherwise the new wine will burst the skins, and it will be spilled out, and the skins will be ruined."

1.   He was ushering in a new life, which was stronger than the old life; and
2.   He could not take His teachings and patch up the old teachings.

The followers of the old system would react violently and quickly. Why? Because they are "holding to a form of godliness, although they have denied its power; and avoid such men as these." (Second Timothy 3:5 NASB).

Many worship traditions of men and not God. His desire is for us to lay hold to the message of reconciliation. He is ready to revive, renew, restore, and empower His church. True religion would have been drastically torn and unstable to clothe a man. Second Corinthians 5:19-20 (NASB) tells us:

> "Namely, that God was in Christ reconciling the world to Himself, not counting their trespasses against them, and He has committed to us the word of reconciliation. Therefore, we are ambassadors for Christ, as though God were entreating through us; we beg you on behalf of Christ, be reconciled to God."

Let the power of God regenerate, equip, favor, dwell, and bless you.

Anointed with Fresh Oil

We come to a place in our walk with the Lord where every day the Lord is pouring fresh oil upon us. "Thou dost prepare a table before me in the presence of my enemies. Thou hast anointed my head with oil; my cup runs overflows" (Ps. 23:5 NASB). In the midst of our enemies, God will strengthen us with all power. Psalm 92:10 (NASB) says, "But Thou hast exalted my horn like that of the wild ox; I have been anointed with fresh oil."

A horn was used to sound a call to declare victory. The horn is an object that symbolizes force and strength. The horn is a hard growth found on the top of the heads of cattle, sheep, rams, and goats. The horn was used as an instrument to call to arms and as a battle sound.

The horn is used to symbolize power, dominion, honor, and glory. His anointing affirms what has been going on in our lives, usually when we have gone through crises and trials. Ask the Lord to transform you with strength and power.

The anointing gives us power, as in Acts 1:8 (NASB) "But you shall receive power when the Holy Spirit has come upon you; and you shall be My witnesses both in Jerusalem, and in all Judaea and Samaria, and even to the remotest part of the earth." The Holy Spirit gives us power to witness for Christ. The anointing makes us grow spiritually. Psalm 92:12-13 (NASB) tells us when God anoints somebody with His Spirit; "The righteous man will flourish like the palm tree, he will grow like a cedar in Lebanon.

Planted in the house of the Lord, they will flourish in the courts of our God." The anointing breaks yokes, as it says in Isaiah 10:27 (NASB), "So it will be in that day, that his burden will be removed from your shoulders and his yoke from your neck, and the yoke will be broken because of fatness." Your yoke shall be broken when you allow the Spirit to have total control over your life. Spiritual yokes (bondages, restraints, and restrictions) are broken and destroyed by the anointing upon the people of God.

Who Am I in Christ?

The Carnal Mind versus the Spiritual Mind

The carnal mind is the mind of the flesh. It means walking according to reasoning dictated by what your five senses (see, hear, touch, smell, feel) are telling you. Romans 8:6 (NASB) "For the mind set on the flesh is death, but the mind set on the Spirit is life and peace" gives us a clear description of each and the results of each. The carnal-minded person has a real dislike for the spiritual things of God.

What does it mean to be carnally minded? To be carnally minded means to cater to the appetites and impulses of one's human nature, which is displeasing to God. Carnally minded is thinking and doing what is right in one's own eyes. Carnally minded means your thought process is generally what you can naturally expect. If you want to get down to the truth of it, to be carnally minded means you have a mindset that is contrary to God and His Word and His will for your life—as well as His planned outcome for you in any situation.

The mind will gravitate toward darkness (carnality) if it is not focused on the Word (Eph. 4:18 NASB "Being darkened in their understanding, excluded from the life of God, because of the ignorance that is in them, because of the hardness of their heart"). Carnally minded people are not able to receive solid food but only milk. When we allow our souls (minds) to agree with the

Word, the body has to submit. But, when the body is leading us, we are being led by what we see, hear, touch, smell, and feel.

Spiritually mind means being led by the Word of God. It enables us to spiritually discern the things of the Spirit of God. "And do not be conformed to this world, but be transformed by the renewing of our mind, that you may prove what the will of God is, that which is good and acceptable and perfect" (Rom. 12:2 NASB). The word transformed means to be changed, and the word renewing means freshness and new. We are changed from the life of the old man to the life of the new man, with Christ's mind. We "exercise" His mind by speaking as Proverbs 18:21 (NASB) says, "death and life are in the power of the tongue."

Jesus is the new man; He is the one with the renewed (fresh) mind; we are to put on (receive) Him and use His mind. God's thoughts differ from man's thoughts.

The mind of Christ and the carnal mind are opposed to one another. Isaiah 55:8 (NASB) tells us: "For My thoughts are not your thoughts, neither are your ways My ways, declares the Lord."

Proverbs 23:7 (NASB) says, "For as he thinks within himself, so he is. He says to you, 'Eat and drink!' But his heart is not with you." How you think is how you will act. If you allow your carnal mind to rule, your ways will be opposite God's ways.

To be spiritually minded means you keep yourself focused on the Word of God. Joshua 1:8 (NASB) declares, "This book of the law shall not depart from your mouth, but you shall meditate on it day and night, so that you may be careful to do according to all that is written in it; for then you will make your way prosperous, and then you will have success."

To be saved, you must know something about God. He is righteous, holy, just, and loving. These are basic facts, revealed in the Bible, that you must know to be saved. You must agree that these facts are true. But watch this, if that is all that saving faith entails, then Satan and the demons are saved. They know these things, and they know that they are true. Saving faith is personally trusting Jesus Christ, committing your eternal destiny to what He did for you on the Cross.

Faith does not mean that God will do whatever you decide you want Him to do. Faith means that you truly believe that God will do what He has already promised to do, and your actions will demonstrate that belief. God gives us many promises in the Bible. Having faith means that we believe them all. And because of our faith, our actions will correspond. We will act on what we believe. Our actions will attest to our faith. The Bible says in James 2:26 (NASB) "For just as the body without the spirit is dead, so also faith without works is dead." If one says he believes, but his life does not correspond to what he says he believes, then he does not believe, no matter how much he argues to the contrary.

You Have Been Chosen as God's Treasured Possession

Isaiah 43:1 (NASB) encourages us: "But now, thus says the Lord, your Creator, O Jacob, and He who formed you, O Israel, do not fear, for I have redeemed you; I have called you by name; you are Mine!" Exodus 23:22 (NASB) tells us: "But if you will truly obey His voice and do all that I say, then I will be an enemy to your enemies and an adversary to your adversaries."

God has brought you forth out of the iron furnace to be unto Him a kingdom of priests. Thus, we can show others the goodness of God, how He brought us from darkness to light, from nothing to something, from rejected to accepted. We cannot accurately represent God to the world if our lives are not holy and set apart.

It took the children of Israel three months of trusting God to get to this place. All that they went through was meant to bring them to this place. This was the beginning of the fulfillment of what God said in Exodus 3:12 (NASB), "And He said, 'Certainly I will be with you, and this shall be the sign to you that it is I who have sent you: when you have brought the people out of Egypt, you shall worship God at this mountain.'"

God had to remove the children of Israel from the idolatry and sin that was present in Egypt in order to have the relationship with them that he wanted. The Egyptians worshipped many gods; this is why it was essential for God to remove the Israelites, so that they could meet the one and only true God.

PART II

The Mandate
(Proving)

Then the Lord stretched out His hand and touched my mouth, and the Lord said to me, "Behold, I have put My words in your mouth. See, I have appointed you this day over the nations and over the kingdoms, to pluck up and to break down, to destroy and to overthrow, to build and to plant." (Jer. 1:9-10 NASB)

CHAPTER 8

TRANSITION INTO YOUR NEW SEASON

Second Corinthians 5:17 (NASB) tells us, "Therefore if any man is in Christ, he is a new creature; the old thing has passed away; behold, new things have come."

Our season of past failures are over. We must shift in this new season. Our mindset must shift and our focus must shift. Everything about us must shift. This is one of the greatest opportunities to go forth and reap the harvest.

The word transition means passing from one condition or place to another. Isaiah 43:19 (NASB) says, "Behold, I will do a something new, now it will spring forth; will you not be aware of it? I will even make a roadway in the wilderness, rivers in the desert."

The drought has broken! God is ready to open up His spiritual rivers of living waters, as Isaiah 41:18-20 (NASB) says,

"I will open rivers on the bare heights, and springs in the midst of the valleys; I will make the wilderness a pool of water, and the dry land fountains of water. I will put the cedar in the wilderness, the acacia, and the myrtle, and the olive tree; I will place the juniper in the desert, together with the box tree and the cypress, that they may see and reorganize, and consider and gain insight as well, that the hand of the Lord has done this, that the Holy One of Israel has created it."

In the same place where the enemy says it's over, I prophesy to that very same place, that you are getting ready to tap into a fresh anointing and a brand-new supply of God's glory and power. That will cause you to rise up with boldness, new faith, and determination.

The Lord of the breakthrough is here. He has broken through your enemy's camp. Your deliverance will cause a bursting out of praise. Seek the Lord for guidance and divine directions. He has opened up the realm of His glory. The new realm is called impact which means to affect, to hit with force. Remove the limits; refuse to be denied access.

God said He will reject anything we offer in this new season that is not properly prepared. It was by faith Abel brought God a better and more acceptable sacrifice than Cain. Hebrews 11:4 (NASB) explains: "By faith Abel offered to God a better sacrifice than Cain, through which he obtained the testimony that he was righteous, God testifying about his gifts, and through faith, though he is dead, he still speaks."

Divine favor falls on us when we present our offerings with the right heart and attitude. Our attitude toward the things of God will play a big part in Him accepting our offerings. This deals with true and false worship before God. It's our approach on how we worship God. In this new season, we will have to teach people how to approach and worship God. Abel knew how to approach God because of what Adam taught him. Cain's worship was false because he was seeking God's acceptance by his own way and by his own hands.

God saw Cain's heart, and rejected his offering. God accepted Abel's offering because it was based on faith. Able sacrificed the firstborn of his flock and understood that he needed God's grace and mercy. So, he made a sacrifice that represented his heart's desire to follow the Lord. His worship was from the heart. Instead of Cain repenting and changing his heart, he stormed off angry, bitter, and jealous.

Worship is a matter of the heart, and what's in it can affect your worship experience with God. There was nothing wrong with the form of Cain's offering (grain); the problem was a matter of the heart. We are taught to go church every Sunday and sing in the choir, thinking that's acceptable worship to God but not realizing the only way we can have a true worship experience with God is through faith.

Faith means to trust or believe in God. It doesn't matter what you sacrifice, if your heart is not right with Him, He cannot and will not accept your offering (worship). God wants our heart and not our lip service or any other false act of worship. Isaiah 29:13 (NASB) proves this, stating, "Then the Lord said,

> 'Because this people draw near with their words and honor Me with their lip service, but they remove their hearts far from Me, and their reverence for Me consists of tradition learned by rote."

Worship is the sacrifice of our life, time, talent, and treasure. True worship is a matter of heart. Cain's problem was not what he brought in his hands, but what he brought in his heart. True worship is understanding who God is and responding to Him. It is an intimate and transparent moment where our hearts are totally unguarded before the Father. Worship is submission to God's will. God wants our hearts. It's great that we come to church, but worship is more than that.

The Transitioning of the Mantle

God unmistakably wants to teach us a lesson through Elijah and Elisha's journey. He wants to do greater things with this generation than He did with the last generation. Elijah represents the older generation. Elisha represents the younger generation. Understand there was a shift in the prophetic era that was about to take place. This shift was going to take what Elijah had done and move it to another level. However, there was a process that had to be done first. Many of us know that in order for you to go from one level to another, one must go through a process. In the shift, those who were not faithful to you in the beginning will not follow you to the end.

When Elijah divided the waters, only Elisha went with him over to dry ground. Most people do not want the mantle; they just want a title. When Elijah dropped his mantle, it was the release of his authority. Romans 13:1 (NASB) declares: "Let every person be in subjection to the governing authorities. For there is no authority except from God, and those which exist are established by God."

A mantle was a loose-fitting official garment of a prophet. It represents spiritual authority and anointing. It was a sure sign of God's endorsement to the prophetic ministry.

Again, most people don't want the mantle; they just want a title. God honors those with an attitude of submission. There are four stages to the process of transitioning the shift of the mantle in 2 Kings Chapter 2:1-6 (NASB) "And it came about when the Lord was about to take up Elijah by a whirlwind to heaven, that Elijah went with Elisha from Gigal. And Elijah said to Elisha, "Stay here please, for the Lord has sent ma as far as Bethel".....And Elijah said to him, "Elisa, please stay here, for the Lord has sent me to Jericho"...Then Elijah said to him, "Please stay here, for the Lord has sent me to the Jordan." At each stage of the journey, Elisha was discouraged from proceeding further, and he was given discouraging news by the sons of the prophets. He knew it was so but remain faithful to his leader.

- Stage 1 (Gilgal)—a place of new beginnings, a place of safety
- Stage 2 (Bethel)—a place of revelation, a place where God became known and where He became big in the eyes of those who worship Him.
- Stage 3 (Jericho)—a place of victory and power. A place to reflect back on all the great things God had done for and through them.
- Stage 4 (Jordan)—a place of death, a place of self-denial, miracles, transitions, and shifting paradigms; the Jordan teaches you how to wait, to have patience, to have faith, and to trust.

God never intended for us as believers to remain stagnant, but He expects our lives to become lives of progression. The young prophets were students of the scripture. They even had some prophetic vision. But something was missing in them—the power, the anointing, and the authority of the Holy Spirit. They could witness, preach, and speak of miracles, but they had not experienced God's power for themselves. God is looking for mantle wearers and anointing carriers in this hour, those who will pick up the mantle and never lay it down.

You can't conquer a place you have never visited. If the man or woman of God doesn't lead or mentor you in the place of your destiny, when the double mantle (anointing) falls upon you, it would become impossible to use, especially if you have not been properly trained. You can operate in power (the ability or potential to do something), but you don't have the authority (legal and formal right to command, enforce orders) to shift, transition, or release miracles in your region or territory.

A shift in the prophetic was about to take place by taking what Elijah had done to another level.

Boundaries are the restricted areas of a prophet's ability to see or believe beyond their experiences in the spiritual realm.

I noticed an important fact: The sons of the prophet tried to discourage Elisha about tagging along with Elijah, but Elisha wouldn't take any part in their discouragement because he was sold out and a committed follower of his leader. The sons of the prophet attempted to bring Elisha down to their level of commitment . What they really were saying is, "Why are you following Elijah? Don't you know that he is a has-been and that God is finished with him and is no longer using him? Why commit your whole life to an old vessel of God? Elisha knew it would take more than commitment and dedication for the double-portion anointing. It takes perseverance in facing discouragement and opposition for the release of the double portion.

The anointing isn't cheap; the power of God comes with a price. Just because Elisha desired to have the anointing wasn't enough. He needed to go the extra mile to receive it. As you can see, there aren't many who will make this journey to obtain the double portion of God's that is best for their lives. Most will only go so far as to watch what happens, to marvel at what God is doing, but then won't commit themselves to be a part of what God is doing for fear that something may be required of them that they aren't willing to do.

Elisha had to be willing to die to his old desires, his old dreams, and his own path that he had chosen. He had to lay down his life for the Lord so God could raise him up and give him the thing which he desired most—the double portion of God's spirit and power.

You will never experience the power of the double portion if you don't step out of your comfort zone.

What does Elisha teach us about the kind of character God wants in leaders and believers? They must have a teachable spirit to learn of experiencing the Lord and His ministry. This candidate must be someone who will be loyal and committed as a servant. Many people are looking for a title but don't want to serve. This means not having a willingness to go the extra mile. Nor are they willing to be devoted to God's calling, God's priorities and goals for your life.

Will you be like the sons of the prophets, those who are under the prophetic teaching of the spirit of Elijah but watch from a distance because they like the message but are not willing to pay the price to become the manifestation of the message?

CHAPTER 9

IGNITING THE FIRE OF EVANGELISM

Is there a stirring within your soul or a fire that has sparked something within you? That something is the Holy Spirit who has caused us to be movers and shakers, making a difference by sharing the love of Jesus. The prophet Isaiah said, "For Zion's sake I will not keep silent, and for Jerusalem's sake I will not keep quiet, until her righteousness goes forth like brightness, and her salvation like a torch that is burning" (Isa. 62:1 NASB).

We can no longer remain silent, and allow evil to continue to triumph. We must unmask the evil ones, by contending for the faith. The message of Jesus Christ is under attack. Jude 3 (NASB) instructs us: "Beloved, while I was making every effort to write you about our common salvation, I felt the necessity to write to you appealing that you contend earnestly for the faith which was once for all delivered to the saints."

This is called the process of return, renewal, and repentance. There is a dew from heaven falling upon the remnant (a small surviving group). Those whose seed will produce peace, prosperity and increase the fruit of their labor. Then people shall inherit and possess all these things. There is an abundance of things to come. Dew from heaven is falling. Haggai 2:9 (NASB) says, "The latter glory of this house will be greater than the former, says the Lord of hosts, 'and in this place I shall give peace,' declares the Lord of hosts."

Consider your ways and thoughtfully reflect on your conduct. The heavens are opened and ready to produce your harvest. The Lord of great prosperity is ready to release the treasures of His house, pouring out new wine and new oil. You will enjoy the fruits of your labor because it was not in vain. Heavenly dew is being released in this now season. God's presence, anointing, and revelation in deeper dimensions are being released. Dimension here is a measurable extent of some kind, such as length, breadth, depth, or height.

Ephesians 3:18-19 (NASB) tells us to:

> "May be able to comprehend with all the saints what is the breadth and length and height and depth, and to know the love of Christ which surpasses knowledge, that you may be filled up to all the fullness of God."

This dew will bring forth healing, miraculous signs, wonders, deeper revelation, and direction to many of our hearts and lives.

Galatians 6:9 (NASB) says, "And let us not lose heart in doing good, for in due time we shall reap if we do not grow weary."

Natural dew is the tiny, glistening drops of water, that often appears on plants and blades of grass early on clear mornings, whereas the dew of God's presence represents strength. Although the dew is a fine mist, it's enough to start softening the hard ground of one's heart. If you notice in the morning when dew falls on plants, it looks withered; then, when the sun begins to rise the plant stands tall and strong. The refreshing dew of the Lord uncovers new supply and reveals new provision of God's abundance.

Seek the Lord

When the hostile enemies gathered against Jehoshaphat and Judah, the nation gathered in prayer to seek God. The word seek means to search for, desire, require, demand. The true purpose of prayer is to bring us into partnership and agreement with the Lord for the fulfillment of His plan and purpose in the earth.

Psalm 105:4 (NASB) says, "Seek the LORD and his strength; seek His face continually." What does it really mean "to seek God"? It means to set your mind and heart on the things of God. First Chronicles 22:19 (NASB) says, "Now set your heart and your soul to seek the Lord your God; arise, therefore, and build the sanctuary of the Lord God, so that you may bring the ark of the covenant of the Lord and the holy vessels of God into the house that is to be built for the name of the Lord." A heart that is set on God has abandoned itself to Him as their one and only.

In Psalm 63:1 (NASB), David cried, "O God, Thou art my God; I shall seek Thee earnestly; My soul thirsts for Thee, my flesh yearns for Thee, in a dry and weary land where there is no water."

"Seek the Lord while He may be found; call upon Him while He is near" Isa. 55:6 (NASB). Search for Him with all your heart. The doors are opened.

Replenishment

There will come a time in life that you feel will drain in your energy, relationships with people, and even ministry. Many people have so many expectations of us and need our attention. How do we find the way and time to combat these draining effects of unending tasks of unmet needs and expectations?

Jesus went for a home visitation, recorded in Mark 1:29 (NASB) "And immediately after they had come out of the synagogue, they came into the house of Simeon and Andrew, with James and John." They ended the day with a large healing and deliverance service, which impacted the community. Preaching such a powerful service can leave you mentally drained, but it didn't stop Jesus from getting up very early in the morning. In a similar situation, most of us would have probably slept in late. He got up early and spent quiet alone time with His Father. He went to a place of solitude. It was between Him and the Father. It wasn't intercession but communion. It wasn't about ministry but a relationship. It was about the sharing of hearts.

It was a time of replenishing. We all need that time with our heavenly Father to refresh our spirit. It helps us to see the bigger picture. It restores our confidence and strength. Communion with God nourishes our spirit.

Solitude with God rejuvenates us. It's a time to share your heart. It's a time of refilling. You have nothing else to give if you don't get refilled. Almost everything in life drains you. Only God can refill, restore, and revive you. He renews your strength. He reenergizes you with His Spirit. He replenishes what you have expended. Time alone with God will help you realign your priorities.

Jehovah Rapha the Lord our healer, shows up when we need Him. In the midst of bitterness and hurt, God reveals Himself as your healer. The word rapha means to restore, to heal, or to cure physically, emotionally, and spiritually.

Sometimes we all need healing in our emotions, physical body, and spiritual mind. David said in Psalm 6:2-3 (NASB), "Be gracious to me, O Lord, for I am pining away; Heal me, O Lord, for my bones are dismayed. And my soul is greatly dismayed; but Thou, O Lord—how long?" Jehovah Rapha will "heal the brokenhearted, and binds up their wounds"(Ps. 147:3 NASB). The word broken means to burst, to break into pieces, to crush, and to smash. Emotional pain can sometimes feel overwhelming. But in the midst of your tears, cry out to Jehovah Rapha and ask Him to put you back together again.

All the healing you need is in the Word of God, and by faith, draw from the healing power of His Word. He sent His Word to heal, as Psalm 107:20 (NASB) states, "He sent His word and healed them, and delivered them from their destructions."

According to Hebrews 4:12 (NASB), His Word is living and active:

> "For the word of God is living and active, and sharper than any two-edged sword, and piercing as far as the division of soul and spirit, and of both joints and marrow, and able to judge the thoughts and intentions of the heart."

God Has Given Us Special Privileges

God has given special privilege to those who have an ear to hear. Jesus was revealing spiritual truth through the parables to those who were sincere seekers because they were the ones who were receptive to the spiritual truth they heard. To others, parables were only stories without any meaning. "The secret things that belong to the Lord our God, but the revealed things belong to us and to our sons forever, that we may observe all the words of this law" (Deut. 29:29 NASB).

God brings revelation to us through: (1) His Holy Spirit—John 16:13 (NASB) "But when He, the Spirit of truth, comes, He will guide you into all the truth; for He will not speak on His own initiative, but whatever He hears, He will speak; and He will disclose to you what is to come"; (2) His prophets—Amos 3:7 (NASB)

"Surely the Lord God does nothing, unless He reveals His secret counsel to His servants the prophets"; and (3) His Word—Joshua 1:8 (NASB) "This book of the law shall not depart from your mouth, but you shall meditate on it day and night, so that you may be careful to do according to all that is written in it; for then you will make your way prosperous, and then you will have good success."

Because of our ignorance, we have limited God. Our moral understanding is darkened, and our reasoning is unclear about the life of God, due to their hardness of heart. When people reject Jesus, the little understanding of the Word of God they have will become useless in their lives. Mark 4:21-25 NASB says, "And He was saying to them, A lamp is not brought to be put under a basket, is it, or under a bed? Is it not brought to be put on the lampstand? For nothing is hidden, except to be revealed; nor has anything been secret, but that it would come to light. If anyone has ears to hear, let him hear. And He was saying to them, Take care what you listen to. By your standard of measurement it will be measured to you; and more will be given you besides. For whoever has to him, more shall be given; and whoever does not have, even what he has shall be taken away from him."

When we walk in disobedience, stubbornness, unforgiveness, it will cause the Light of Jesus to become dim in our lives. As a result, others will not be able to see the Jesus we are talking about, because there is no light shining in our lives.

God's truth is revealed, not hidden. It is our responsibility to not only hear God, but to be receptive to what we are hearing. There are four types of hearers described in Matthew 13:3-9 (AMP): (1) Those who hear without understanding (easy to forget, and easy for Satan to snatch away what they have heard); (2) Those who hear with their emotions (and are easy to backslide); (3) Those who hear carelessly (still stuck in their worldly ways); and (4) This who hear with understanding (and produce fruit). Those who produce fruit will be strong, stable and immovable.

Hearers do not just hear but watch and wait for the Word of the Lord to be manifested in abundance over their lives. Proverbs 8:34 (NASB) assures us that "Blessed is the man who listens to me, watching daily at my gates, waiting at my doorposts."

Deuteronomy 29:29 (NASB) says that "The secret things belong to the Lord our God, but the things which are revealed belong to us and to our sons forever, that we may observe all the words of this law."

We Must Arise Above the Average

God has given us three things: time, talent, and treasure to use according to our abilities. The issue is not how much we have, but how well we use it.

An "average servant" is a bit self-seeking, a little materialistic. Most of his daily choices are about improving his life. They are about self-improvement, and not kingdom improvement, and they can drain a believer of their spiritual power. They are powerless and lack self-sacrifice. In other words, it's all about them.

They make up excuses on why they are not doing what the Lord Jesus has called them to do.

But how many of us know that God is raising up a remnant of people who will not shrink back from truth of His Word? There shall be a supernatural regathering of God's people. Jeremiah 23:3 (NASB) confirms this, "Then I Myself shall gather the remnant of My flock out of all the countries where I have driven them and shall bring them back to their pastures; and they will be fruitful and multiply."

We have to arise above the average to proclaim Christ's gospel without fear or hindrance. Let's pray: "Lord, I am an empty vessel; fill me and lead me where You would have me to go as your witness. In Jesus's name. Amen."

It's Time to Give Satan His Letter of Deportation

Deportation—the act or an instance of expulsion of an undesirable alien from a country.

The reason for deportation: (1) Satan enters a ministry illegally by using false representation of being a citizen of the kingdom of God. It's when his passport date has expired and his visa is invalid; (2) he violates his status during the stay, which means he worked without proper authorization or overstayed the permitted authorization period of status giving by God; (3) he falsified documents claiming to be a citizen of the kingdom of God; (4) he unlawfully tried to become permanent resident; and (5) he committed aggravated felonies at his time of admission. So, therefore, by the power and authority given to us by Jesus Christ the Son of the living God, you can therefore deport him from your ministry. Luke 4:1-3 (NASB) "And Jesus, full of the Holy Spirit, returned from the Jordan and was led about by the Spirit in the wilderness for forty days, being tempted by the devil. And He ate nothing during those days; and when they had ended, He became hungry. And the devil said to Him, "If You are the Son of God, tell this stone to become bread."" This shows us that Jesus wasn't tempted in the temple but in the wilderness where He was tired, alone, hungry, and thus, most vulnerable. The devil often tempts us when we are vulnerable.

The devil's temptations focused on three crucial areas according to First John 2:15-16: the lust of the flesh (physical needs and desires), the lust of the eyes (possessions and power), and the pride of life (obsession with one's status or importance).

Eviction—is a legal process by which a landlord or owner may seek the eviction of his or her tenants; the removal of a tenant from possession of premises in which he or her resides.

There is a Difference Between Speaking Engagements and Apostolic Assignments

A speaking engagement is a planned event in which an individual educates an audience on a particular topic. In marketing, speaking engagements are used to increase a client's visibility and strengthen his or her reputation as an expert in that field.

An apostolic assignment is a task, or piece of work assigned to someone to promote God's divine order; to gather, equip, and build up the kingdom of God for His divine purpose.

CHAPTER 10

OUR KINGDOM AUTHORITY

I was fasting and praying, and it seemed like there was no result to my prayer. I asked the Lord why? He said because I had not used my legal authority by taking dominion over the spirit of fear. Colossians 1:13-14 (NASB) says: "For He delivered us from the domain of darkness, and transferred us to the kingdom of His beloved Son, in whom we have redemption, the forgiveness of sins." God has given us authority to take dominion over the power of darkness.

A kingdom key is found in Luke 10:19 (NASB): "Behold, I have given you authority to tread upon serpents and scorpions, and over all the power of the enemy, and nothing shall injure you."

Dominion is defined as control or power over, or the authority to rule. To take dominion means you have the power or right of governing and controlling with God's sovereign authority. When you are in charge of something, or rule it, you have dominion over it. It's called legal authority.

Many of us are speaking the Word of God but are not speaking it in the name of Jesus, without power and authority. James 1:6 (NASB) instructs, "But let him ask in faith, without any doubting, for the one who doubts is like the surf of the sea driven and tossed by the wind."

Matthew 16:19 (NASB) tells us: "I will give you the keys of the kingdom of heaven; and whatever you shall bind on earth shall be bound in heaven, and whatever you shall loose on earth shall be loosed in heaven." Binding and loosing are the keys to victory in every difficulty we face as believers. We have dominion over the challenges that have troubled our minds. We can exercise dominion over every spirit that tries to break the peace of God in our life and in our home. We can boldly declare that every generational curse that hinders our flow in Christ is nullified in the name of Jesus, and we can declare that every spirit contrary to the Spirit of Christ is under subjection.

The Lord kept sending His Word to me, found in Isaiah 41:10 (KJV)"Fear thou not; for I am with thee: be not dismayed; for I am thy God: I will strengthen Thee; yea, I will help thee; I will uphold thee with the right hand of my righteousness." Dismayed means very upset, disappointed, or annoyed about something surprising or shocking that has happened.

We can boldly declare that the weapons of the enemy shall have no effect on us. We can break every tormenting effect fear had over our lives. Proverbs 28:1 (NLT) reminds us: "The wicked run away when no one is chasing them, but the godly are as bold as lions."

We can boldly reject every form of satanic destruction and break free from them. Our life is anointed to carry out the will and purpose of God. Isaiah 54:17 (NASB) declares: "No weapon that is formed against you shall prosper; and every tongue that accuses you in judgment you will condemn. This is the heritage of the servants of the Lord. And their vindication is from Me, declares the Lord."

By faith we are to confess that we are victorious and everything we touch and do will carry the mark of God's blessing. We confess boldly that every pit that the enemy has dug for our life will become a stepping stone, and that God, who promoted Joseph from a prison to palace, is with us. God Himself will promote us in the midst of adversity to possess the land. The horn of our strength shall be exalted, and the grace of God shall abound in our lives for all eyes to see. Yes, God's plan is to prosper us and not to harm us. God's plan is to elevate us and not to demote us. First Corinthians 2:9 (KJV) tells us, "But as it is written, eye hath not seen, ear hath not heard, neither have entered into the heart of man, the things which God hath prepared for them that love him"

The joy of the Lord is our strength, which causes favor and blessings to flow toward us. The favor of the Lord goes everywhere with us. And the Lord's blessing is manifested, even in adverse situations. The eye of the Lord goes with us and causes us to stand before kings and to have favor with all men. According to God's Word to Deuteronomy 28:7 (NASB) "The LORD will cause your enemies who rise up against you to be defeated before you; they shall come out against you one way and shall flee before you seven ways." Satan no longer has authority over believers, unless they give him access. We are to praise God for His goodness and mercy and for the increase of blessing and favor. This is our time and season of increase.

God's Divine Gift to those who have been faithful. Psalm 90:17 (NASB) declares: "And let the favor of the Lord our God be upon us; and do confirm for us the work of our hands; yes, confirm the work of our hands."

Soundness of mind is a gift from God; it is the fruit which comes from the Word of God, and it gives peace in the time of trouble, power in the time of struggle, and love in the time of conflict. When you possess the Word of God in your heart, then you will have the power of a sound mind.

First Peter 1:13 (NASB) says, "Therefore, gird your mind for action, keep sober in spirit; fix your hope completely on the grace to be brought to you at the revelation of Jesus Christ." The mind is protected when you fill it with God's Word. Proverbs 4:20-21 (NASB) tells us: "My son, give attention to my words; incline your ear to my sayings. Do not let them depart from your sight; keep them in the midst of your heart."

Therefore, we must receive, meditate, and memorize His promises, and apply its principles to our life. Until we place a demand on the Word of God, nothing in our lives will change. "Now to Him who is able to do exceeding abundantly beyond all that you ask or think, according to the power that works within us" (Eph.

3:20 NASB). He requires that you release the power of His Word by speaking it with your mouth. Speak the Word only.

Through faith, you can call these promises from the spiritual realm to the natural. Faith is the revealed evidence of God's kingdom in power and action.

Jesus told His disciples, "Behold, I give unto you power to tread on serpents and scorpions, and over all the power of the enemy: and nothing shall by any means hurt you" (Luke 10:19 KJV). This is the authority we have in Christ Jesus, and it is activated by faith. You will never be able to exercise authority you don't believe you possess. The moment we press beyond our feelings and emotions in order to engage God in prayer is the moment you will begin experiencing the supernatural turnaround that you long anticipated.

> Daniel 10:12–13 (NASB) says, "Then he said to me, 'Do not be afraid, Daniel, for from the first day that you set your heart on understanding this and on humbling yourself before your God, your words were heard, and I have come in response to your words. But the prince of the kingdom of Persia was withstanding me for twenty-one days; then behold, Michael, one of the chief princes, came to help me, for I had been left there with the kings of Persia.'"

You must take authority over the "spirit of opposition" right now. If you notice, the heavenly being who revealed himself to Daniel told him that his prayer was heard from the very first day, but that while he was en route to reach Daniel with the answer to his prayer, the prince of the Kingdom of Persia withstood Him. Who is this prince? It was a demonic principality assigned to the region of Persia. This demonic principality was responsible for hindering or preventing prayers from being answered. This is what we call a "spirit of opposition" a demonic force that seeks to hinder the manifestation of prayers, prophecies, breakthroughs, and progress in the life of believers.

If you have ever felt strong spiritual opposition when you were doing something God called you to do, it was because the spirit of opposition was interfering. The spirit of opposition tries to discourage believers by hindering the promises of God from manifesting in their lives. If the ministry is not growing or experiencing the blessings and provision that we knew God had ordained for us, then you are dealing with a spirit of opposition. To deal with it, we must do what God did in the beginning of creation. When there was void and darkness, He spoke the Word and commanded the light to come forth.

Take authority over this hindering spirit and declare the promises of God's Word over your Church. Say, "In the name of Jesus Christ, let there be light." You need to address the spiritual forces that are preventing your Church from moving in its full potential. You must take authority over the spirit of opposition right now.

Too many believers are sitting around, waiting for something to happen while they suffer unnecessarily. This is nothing more than a device of the enemy. Lay hold of God's promises now. Say, "I declare that the counsel of the devil is confused, in Jesus' name. I declare that no weapon formed against you shall prosper." Take dominion over the powers of darkness. No longer will we allow Satan to buffet us while we behave like victims. Stand up, in Jesus's name.

CHAPTER 11

THE HIDDEN WARRIORS OF GOD

God has given us a mandate to go and prepare the Body of Christ. We are the hidden warriors who were waiting for the time of God's manifestation. God has reserved us for such as a time as this. Therefore, He is calling out those whom have prepared themselves in secret, hidden away in preparation for their time of manifestation to the world.

Judges 6:11-12 (NASB) "Then the Angel of the Lord came and sat under the oak that was in Ophrah, which belonged to Joash the Abiezrite, as his son Gideon was beating out wheat in the wine press in order to save it from the Midianites. And the Angel of the Lord appeared to him and said to him, The Lord is with you, O valiant warrior" shows us that Gideon was the hidden warrior. He was hiding from the Midianites who had taken control of Israel. Gideon was bullied by the enemy, and he could not seem to get ahead. An Angel of the Lord appeared to Gideon and said, "The Lord is with thee," and Gideon's response was, "If the

Lord be with us, why then is all this befallen us?" And he probably wondered, where are all His miracles?

God has given us authority in the earth. We are the ones to exercise that authority each and every day by resisting the enemy and enforce the victory of Jesus over him. Judges 6:14 (NASB) says, "And the Lord looked at him said, Go in this your strength and deliver Israel from the hand of Midian. Have I not sent you?" Gideon was given power because of his position. We are filled with power of God. It is activated by our words and actions of faith upon our covenant rights.

"Have I not sent you?" The Lord did not say I am sending you, but have I not already sent you? This is a covenant. Gideon was to stand up with his covenant rights and demand his land back in the name of the Lord and route out those uncircumcised Midianites who had no covenant with God.

The enemy has stolen land from many Christians. They are waiting on God to do something about it. They are hiding in their wine presses, waiting for miracles to take place and have their land returned to them. It is not going to happen. When you start speaking and walking in faith, the miracles will start to manifest, and the enemy will flee.

Before Gideon could become Israel's deliverer, he had to first come to know God in a very real, personal, and reverent way. One of the most important keys to serving God is to know Him well and to have a right relationship with Him.

God used evil oppressors to punish the Israelites for their sins, to bring them to the point of repentance. We are in the season of repentance. When God gives you a mission, you must not abandon it. The reason for the Israelites' rapid decline was sin, individually and corporately. The Israelites refused to eliminate the enemy completely from the land. This led to idolatry, which led them in doing everything that seemed right to them. Before long, they became captives. Out of their desperation, they begged God to rescue them. In God's faithfulness to His promise and out of His loving kindness, God would raise up a judge to deliver His people. Then, complacency and disobedience would set in, and the cycle would begin again. The gradual deterioration of our relationship with God is often due to the sins we fail to drive out of our lives.

Knowledge Is the Key to a Kingdom Mindset

Why was the knowledge of the secret of the kingdom given to the disciples? It is because they were Christ followers. They listened. They believed. They wanted more. They could never get enough of His teachings.

His disciples were able to harvest the spiritual information that was contained in the parables. Don't you realize that knowledge is something that is not just handed to you? There is something that must transpire on your part in order for you to attain spiritual knowledge and understanding. You must seek and call on God without excuses, Romans 1:20 NASB tells us: "For since the creation of the world His invisible attributes, His eternal power and divine nature, have been clearly seen, being understood through what has been made, so that they are without excuse." We are without excuse. The keys to the kingdom lies in the knowledge of the secrets of the kingdom. Matthew 13:11 (NASB) informs us:

"And He answered and said to them, 'to you it has been granted to know the mysteries of the kingdom of heaven, but to them it has not been granted." The knowledge we have is of the blessings of the kingdom. Matthew 13:16 NASB tells us: "But blessed are your eyes, because they see; and your ears, because they hear." The word see means "to behold." We have revelation knowledge of the kingdom, the secret things of the kingdom. We have knowledge of the blessings in the kingdom. Now God wants us to have a knowledge of the message of the kingdom.

"My people are destroyed for lack of knowledge; because you have rejected knowledge, I also will reject you from being My priest. Since you have forgotten the law of your God, I also will forget your children" (Hos. 4:6 NASB), but Jesus is building His church, and He has given us the keys to the kingdom.

Understanding the Mind of Christ

We can't be expected to renew our minds if we don't really know how. Satan tries to keep us from being transformed, from truly "exchanging our lives," with Christ. Psalm 51:6 (KJV) tells us: "Behold, thou desirest truth in the inward parts: and in the hidden part thou shalt make me to know wisdom." Those inward parts are the center of all righteousness within us. Second Corinthians

5:17-18 (NASB) says, "Therefore, if anyone is in Christ, he is a new creature; the old things passed away; behold, new things have come. Now all these things are from God, who reconciled us to Himself through Christ and gave us the ministry of reconciliation."

Matthew 15:9 (NASB) teaches us: "But in vain do they worship Me, teaching as doctrines the precepts of men." It is vain for any man to profess relationship with Christ according to the flesh, while he is unchanged in the heart and life, and dead in trespasses and sin. God want us free from ourselves, from our circumstances, and from the enemy's involvement so that we are able to serve Him unburdened and in love.

Our mind is not just our conscience thoughts, our intellect, or our brain, but a whole conceptual process, which is a measurable knowledge of information received with a specific concept. In other words, what are you doing with the information you receive, and how are you going to apply it to your circumstances?

Our mind begins with the spirit that resides at the core of our being. That spirit creates the thoughts of our hearts, which in turn produce the actions of our lives. This whole process is called our "mind."

Only the mind of Christ is a divine process of thinking. It is God's Holy Spirit that creates God's supernatural thoughts in our hearts and through a process (again by His Spirit) produces those thoughts as godly actions in our lives. It's the Holy Spirit's mission—with our consent—to produce this mind in us so that we can live the truth in passing the Gospel on to others. The mind of Christ, therefore, is simply a process to where the Word of God becomes a living reality in our lives. God's supernatural thoughts are produced in our lives by His supernatural power.

The Holy Spirit works with us to lead us to Christ; He comes in us to indwell us permanently. John 14:26 (NASB) says: "But the Helper, the Holy Spirit, whom the Father will send in My name, He will teach you all things, and bring to your remembrance all that I said to you." He comes upon us for a supernatural empowering to be His witness and continually refills us so that God's life can continue to flow from our hearts and into our lives.

Being born again refers to receiving the Spirit of God into our hearts; hearts; 1 Peter 1:3 (NASB) tells us: "Blessed be the God and Father of our Lord Jesus Christ, who according to His great mercy has caused us to be born again to a living hope through the resurrection of Jesus Christ from the dead." The Baptism of the Holy Spirit refers to the initial infilling of our souls with the Spirit of God for empowerment; Acts 1:8 (NASB) teaches us: "But you shall receive power when the Holy Spirit has come upon you; and you shall be My witnesses both in Jerusalem, and in all Judea and Samaria, and even to the remotest part of the earth." Refilling refers to the daily filling of our cleansed souls with God's love, wisdom and power; 2 Corinthians 4:16 (NASB) confirms this: "Therefore we do not lose heart, but though our outer man is decaying, yet our inner man is being renewed day by day." This is the fullness of Christ—experiencing His life in place of our own.

This process by the Holy Spirit does not automatically occur; only as we, moment by moment, renew our minds by changing the way we think. Then, we are able to receive from the Holy Spirit. If we choose not to renew our minds, we will quench God's Spirit, and once again His mind and His love will be blocked from our hearts. First Thessalonians 5:19 (NASB) tells us: "Do not quench the Spirit."

Are You a Vessel God Can Use?

Sanctification is the process of being made holy, resulting in a changed lifestyle for the believer. The result of sanctification is glory, the manifestation of God's presence. Glory is symbolized by a fire that does not consume. We need to be careful on how we approach our Lord. His glory was a visible pillar of cloud and fire hovering above the Holy of Holies. Exodus 3:5 (NASB) says, "Then He said, 'Do not come near here; remove your sandals from your feet, for the place on which you are standing is holy ground.'" How do you come into the presence of God? Do you come to Him in humility, reverencing that He is the holy God or arrogant, puffed up in pride, like you are doing God a favor by coming? Moses remove his sandals and covered his face as an act of reverence before a holy God.

If you profess Christ as your Lord and personal Savior, you ought to pursue sanctification, consecration, and holiness because without it, you cannot see the glory of the Lord. God will judge any person claiming identification with Christ while they are not in pursuit of sanctification.

"Not everyone who says to Me, 'Lord, Lord,' will enter the kingdom of heaven, but he who does the will of My Father who is in heaven will enter. Many will say to Me on that day, "Lord, Lord, did we not prophesy in Your name, and in Your name cast out demons, and in Your name perform many miracles?" And then I will declare to them, "I never knew you; depart from Me, you who practice lawlessness" (Matt. 7:21-23 NASB).

You can sound religious but have no personal relationship with Him. It is not what we say that makes us religious but what we believe in our hearts. It's our faith and lifestyle. God calls his own to set them apart. Second Corinthians 7:1 (NLT) informs us: "Because we have these promises, dear friends, let us cleanse ourselves from everything that can defile our body or spirit. And, let us work toward complete purity because we fear God."

Keep Your Mind Focused on the Promise

"Better is the end of a thing than the beginning thereof, and the patient in spirit is better than the proud in spirit" (Eccles. 7:8 KJV).

It is always the end that matters and not how we begin. Time is not measured by the passing of years but by what one does, and what one achieves. It is our attitude that matters to reach or aim for the desired end. Philippians 2:5 (NASB) says, "Have this attitude in yourselves which was also in Christ Jesus."

Not only does our attitude matter, mindset matters to reach the desired end. Romans 12:2 (NASB) tells us, "And do not be conformed to this world, but be transformed by the renewing of your mind, that you may prove what the will of God is, that which is good and acceptable and perfect."

We must keep our mind focused on the promises of God, for in Him we will find strength as we follow Jesus with our whole heart and mind. Galatians 6:9 (KJV) says, "And let us not be weary in well doing; for in due season, we shall reap, if we faint not."

Who Will Stand in the Gap?

"I searched for a man among them who would build up the wall and stand in the gap before Me for the land, so that I would not destroy it; but I found no one" (Eze. 22:30 NASB). The watchman anointing is upon us. To watch means to look out, guard, protect, observe carefully or get a new scope on something, to see an approaching danger and warn those endangered.

There is a difference between a watchman and an intercessor. Watchmen stand their watch in prayer and report to those in authority all they see and hear in the realm of the Spirit. Intercessors stand in the gap and repair the breaches or wall.

God has anointed watchmen with the divine enablement to:

1. SEE—Isaiah 52:8 (NASB) says: "Listen! Your watchmen lift up their voices, they shout joyfully together; for they will see with their own eyes when the LORD restores Zion."

2. HEAR—Proverbs 8:32-34 (NASB) says: "Now therefore, O sons, listen to me, for blessed are they who keep my ways. Heed instruction and be wise, and do not neglect it. Blessed is the man who listens to me, watching daily at my gates, waiting at my doorposts."

3. DISCERNMENT—First John 4:1 (NASB) says: "Beloved, do not believe every spirit, but test the spirits to see whether they are from God; because many false prophets have gone out into the world."

The watchman needs these three weapons in his or her arsenal: the Bible, a concordance, and a commentary. The watchman's anointing allows us to pray against Satan's schemes and plans. It is a vital aspect of our intercession.

Both of these scriptures challenge us to alertness and watchfulness, not only for ourselves, but for our families and ministry. Ephesians 6:18 (NASB) exhorts, "With all prayer and petition pray at all times in the Spirit, and with this in view, be on the alert with all perseverance, and petition for all the saints." First Peter 5:8 (NASB) says, "Be of sober spirit, be on the alert. Your adversary, the devil, prowls about like a roaring lion, seeking someone to devour."

Be on alert, stand firm in your faith "to keep Satan from getting the advantage over us; for we are not ignorant of his wiles and intentions" (2 Cor. 2:11 AMP). Be firm and sure in your prayer request without wavering or doubting that God will answer you.

God is calling the remnants, the ones who will not be shaken by what they see. Those who will stand their watch in prayer, removing every obstacle and stumbling block in the realm of the spirit. Preparing a path for the lost and broken-hearted.

As a watchman for the Lord, you must never keep silent, keep praying and calling out to the Lord for Him to remember His promises to his church. Don't hold your tongue until the church becomes "the light of the world, a city set on an hill cannot be hidden" (Matt. 5:14 AMP). God is not a secret to be kept. We must become light bearers; stop hiding the God you serve. He is the almighty, all-powerful, all-knowing, wonderful Counselor and Prince of Peace.

Foreign countries will see your righteousness, and world leaders your glory. The doors of the Lord are open to all. Acts 13:46 (NASB) confirm this:

> "And Paul and Barnabas spoke out boldly, and said, "It was necessary that the word of God should be spoken to you first; since you repudiate it, and judge yourselves unworthy of eternal life, behold, we are turning to the Gentiles."

Stand your ground by declaring the Word of God, concerning salvation. First Timothy 2:4 (NASB) gives us God's heart, "Who desires all men to be saved and to come to the knowledge of the truth." "The Lord is not slack concerning his promise, as some men count slackness; but is longsuffering to us-ward, not willing that any should perish, but that all should come to repentance" (2 Pet. 3:9 KJV).

Repentance is a transformative change of heart, sincere regret or remorse, to turn from sin, sorrow and regret, and it's more than just feeling bad. One must make a complete change of direction toward God. Repentance is a cleansing agent you must submit to before you can become a vessel God can use. "Because we have these promises, dear friends, let us cleanse ourselves from everything that can defile our body or spirit. And let us work toward complete holiness because we fear God" (2 Cor. 7:1 NLT).

God has given us holy boldness to declare His Word to all who are ready to receive His salvation and righteousness because of our faith in Him. "Let us draw near with a sincere heart in full assurance of faith, having our hearts sprinkled clean from an evil conscience and our bodies washed with pure water. Let us hold fast the confession of our hope without wavering, for He who promised is faithful; and let us consider how to stimulate one another to love and good deeds, not forsaking our own assembling together, as is the habit of some, but encouraging one another; and all the more, as you see the day drawing near" (Heb. 10:22-25 NASB).

A true Watchman is a weapon, striking like an arrow into the heart of the enemy. As a watchman of the Lord, lift up your voice and shout joyfully together until the Lord restores America. The King's favor is toward a servant who acts wisely.

Be on guard, Be alert!

"Devote yourselves to prayer, keeping alert in it with an attitude of thanksgiving; praying at the same time for us as well, that God may open up to us a door for the word, so that we may speak forth the mystery of Christ, for which I have also been imprisoned; in order that I may make it clear in the way I ought to speak. Conduct yourselves with wisdom toward outsiders, making the most of the opportunity. Let your speech always be with grace, seasoned, as it were, with salt, so that you may know how you should respond to each person" (Col.4:2-6 NASB).

1. Maintain the Spirit of Prayer (Be fervent in prayer)

Romans 8:26-27 (NASB) says, "And in the same way the Spirit also helps us in our weakness, for we do not know how to prayer as we should, but the Spirit Himself intercedes for us with groanings too deep for words; and He who searches the hearts knows what the mind of the Spirit is because He intercedes for the saints according to the will of God."

2. Watch for Favorable Opportunities (Pray that God will open a door for His Word to go forth)

Colossians 4:3 (NASB) states, "Praying at the same time pray for us as well, that God may open up to us a door for the word, so that we may speak forth the mystery of Christ, for which I have also been imprisoned."

3. Be Always on Your Guard (Watch and stand fast in faith)

First Peter 5:8 (NASB) says, "Be of sober spirit, be on the alert. Your adversary, the devil, prowls about like a roaring lion, seeking someone to devour."

4. Be Always Grateful to God—who has called you and afford you such abundant means and opportunities to glorify him. (Give thanks to the Lord for every good and perfect gift)

Colossians 3:17 (NASB) says, "And whatever you do in word or deed, do all in the name of the Lord Jesus, giving thanks through Him to God the Father."

5. Devote Yourselves to Prayer (Consecrated to a purpose; dedicated)

Ephesians 6:18 (NASB) tells us to "With all prayer and petition pray at all times in the Spirit, and with this view, be on the alert with all perseverance and petition for all the saints."

Ask God to help you be on guard to overcome the schemes of the devil. Ephesians 6:11 (NASB) says, "Put on the full armor of

God, that you may be able to stand firm against the schemes of the devil."

"See to it that no one takes you captive through philosophy and empty deception, according to the tradition of men, according to the elementary principles of the world, rather than according to Christ" (Col. 2:8 NASB). "Devote yourselves to prayer, keeping alert in it with an attitude of thanksgiving" (Col. 4:2 NASB).

Areas of Alertness:

- Pray that you don't enter into temptation.
- Pray that you remain strong and steadfast in the faith.
- Pray that you remain sober, and don't spiritually fall sleep.
- Pray that you're alert, watching for Satan, his schemes, and his deception.

CHAPTER 12

REVISITING YOUR SPIRITUAL FOUNDATION

"And why do you call Me, 'Lord, Lord,' and do not do what I say? Everyone who comes to Me and hears My words and acts upon them, I will show you whom he is like: he is like a man building a house, who dug deep and laid a foundation on the rock; and when a flood rose, the torrent burst against that house and could not shake it, because it had been well built. But the one who has heard and has not acted accordingly, is like a man who built a house upon the ground without any foundation; and the torrent burst against it and immediately collapsed, and the ruin of that house was great" (Lk. 6:46-49 NASB).

What are foundations? It's the beginning, the core of something. It's the natural or prepared ground or base on which some structures rest. A foundation is also the establishment of an institution with provisions for future maintenance; the basis in which a thing stands, is founded, or is supported; the basis or groundwork of anything.

The church is "built upon the foundation of the apostles and prophets, Christ Jesus himself being the chief corner stone" (Eph. 2:20 KJV). Before God sends His reviving fire upon the church today, He will raise up and empower men and women who will first rebuild the broken-down altar of the Lord and put the church back in its proper order. There are too many people rightly crying out for God to send revival, but it is important to understand that before God can send His revival, He must restore the church to her original state. True revival comes after restoration. God is a God of order, and He must set things in order before He can breathe His life into His church. Restoration involves the work of repairing, fixing, mending, rebuilding, remodeling, revamping, and making things over again.

God is restoring His church to His original intention for her. When God lights up His fire, it burns until everything turns to ashes. He doesn't just light up the fire because the people want the fire; He lights His fire when the people are ready, in unity, with one mind, one voice, and one sound for setting the world on fire for Him. Where there is no altar, there is no fire of the Holy Spirit.

Fire is a symbol of God's purifying presence. He had to purify these disciples first and burn away the undesirable elements in their lives and set their hearts a flame to ignite the lives of the people in Jerusalem, Judea, Samaria, and the ends of the earth.

The body of Christ has shifted into one of the greatest seasons of revival fire. It is called a spiritual awakening. It's a committed focus that builds a foundation of agreement in prayer for breakthroughs over cities and regions. Spiritual awakening takes place when the Sovereignty of God pours out His Spirit to impact a nation.

This is where His Spirit brings restoration and healing upon the land. In Second Chronicles 7:13-15 NASB it states,

> "If I shut up the heavens so that there is no rain, or if I command the locust to devour the land, or if I send pestilence among My people, and My people who are called by My name humble themselves and pray and seek My face and turn from their wicked ways, then I will hear from heaven, will forgive their sin and will heal their land. Now My eyes will be open and My ears attentive to the prayer offered in this place."

In Ephesians 5:14 (NASB) tells us, "Awake, sleeper, and arise from the dead, and Christ will shine on you." Pray that the eyes of your heart be enlightened. Why? Because many have fallen asleep spiritually. Their spiritual senses have become dull and cold to the things of God. First Thessalonians 5:6 (NASB) declares, "So then let us not sleep as others do, but let us be alert and sober."

Believers must take advantage of this opportunity to serve the Lord, "and let us not lose heart in doing good, for in due time we will reap, if we do not grow weary" (Gal. 6:9 NASB). When the power of hidden darkness seeks to enslave us as Pharaoh did in the Old Testament, the Lamb of God, our great deliver and redeemer covers our doorpost with His blood. Be on guard, follow the leading of the Holy Spirit, and shepherd the flocks. "God is our refuge and strength, a very present help in trouble" (Ps. 46:1 NASB).

Hindering Spirits

Hindering spirits, distract, discourage, and try to keep your mouth shut. You must go to war with the Word of God against all hindering spirits. Luke 10:19 (NASB) says, "Behold, I have given you authority to tread upon serpents and scorpions, and over all the power of the enemy, and nothing shall injure you." We have a lot of people operating in the power without authority. Power is the ability or capacity to do something or act in a particular way; the ability to produce an effect. They have the power of speech that will cause people to react and respond a certain way.

God gives strength to the weary and increases their power. Authority is the power or right to give orders, make decisions, and enforce obedience; the authorization of an officer or a messenger to carry out a specific task.

In Luke 9:1 (NASB), "And He called the twelve together, and gave them power and authority over all the demons, and to heal diseases." These are two important words in the kingdom of God. Luke's version of the sending of the disciples is a key passage to understand how authority and power apply to us.

Power (dunamis) has its foundation in the idea of being anointed, while authority (exousia) has its foundation in the concept of being sent out.

Jesus expelled demons by His authority. Romans 8:31 (NASB) tells us: "What then shall we say to these things? If God is for us, who is against us?" The enemy's plan is always to seize you with the spirit of fear, but "God hath not given us the spirit of fear, but of power, and of love, and of a sound mind" (2 Tim. 1:7 KJV).

First Peter 5:8 (NASB) says, "Be of sober spirit, be on the alert. Your adversary, the devil, prowls about like a lion roaring lion, seeking someone to devour." God is closing "demonic doors." This is very important, First Corinthians 10:13 (NASB) assures us,

> "No temptation has overtaken you but such as is common to man; and God is faithful, who will not allow you to be tempted beyond what you are able, but with the temptation will provide the way of escape also, that you may be able to endure it."

Rely totally upon the power of the Word of God. In this new season, we can't go by what we see, hear, touch, smell, or taste. We must believe, trust, know, and have confidence in God and

His Word. Remove the spiritual hindrances of unbelief and discouragement.

The Lord is our strength and our shield; our heart must trust in Him. So, therefore, let our heart greatly rejoice and sing praises to Him. "Let every valley be lifted up, and every mountain and hill be made low; and let the rough ground become a plain, and the rugged terrain a broad valley" (Isa. 40:4 NASB). Your divine helper is here. Your divine support is here. God's divine presence is here. "So that we may boldly say, The Lord is my helper, and I will not fear what man shall do unto me" (Heb. 13:6 NASB).

Come Out with Your Hands Up

Where can we hide? Nowhere. God's all-seeing eye and all-pervading presence keeps close watch on our every moment. He carefully observe our character, thoughts, and words. Colossians 3:17 (NASB) inspires us: "And whatever you do in word or deed, do all in the name of the Lord Jesus, giving thanks through Him to God the Father." We are always surrounded by His power, and never can escape His Word. God's thorough knowledge of us and all our ways are protected by His creative power. Have you ever tried to run away from God? Don't try it; it can't be done.

"Where can I go from Thy Spirit? Or where can I flee from Thy presence?" (Ps. 139:7 NASB). Perhaps you didn't realize that you are being pursued. There is a voice calling you. It is the voice of your Father, your Creator. No matter where we go, the will of God will be there. God is everywhere and sees everything. Rather than flee from Him, we should flee to Him. "God is our refuge and strength, a very present help in trouble" (Ps. 46:1 NASB).

"For I am convinced that neither death, nor life, nor angels, nor principalities, nor things present, nor things to come, nor powers, nor height, nor depth, nor any other created thing, shall be able to separate us from the love of God, which is in Christ Jesus our Lord" (Rom. 8:38-39 NASB). God promises to never leave you nor forsake you. The next time you go through dark days, remember that God knows your problems and needs. Just take refuge in Him; He will see you through.

Whatever difficulties you may be facing, don't hide from it—hide in the Lord. He will give you strength to fight the battle.

Five Demonic Spirits That Attack the Apostolic/Prophetic Move of God

Put your feet on the neck of your enemies.

1). Spirit of Jezebel—(Adoni-Zedek, King of Jerusalem). This demonic spirit leads to injustice, fear, poverty, confusion, and defeat.

2). Spirit of Python & Cobra—(Hogan, King of Hebron). This demonic spirit causes an inability to move forward in the things of God and will always resist spiritual warfare.

3). Spirit of Sabotage—(Piram, King of Jarmuth). This demonic spirit darkens your spiritual understanding, bringing a lack of joy and feeling of bondage.

4). Spirit of Goliath—(Japhia, King of Lachish). This demonic spirit lead to barrenness and isolation. It wants to keep you bridled and too proud to submit to true spiritual authority.

5). Spirit of Opposition—(Debir, King of Elgon). This demonic spirit seeks to get you to attack others' reputation, to bring discredit to leaders, and to stop true prophetic revelation from going forth, or to release false prophets.

This demonic spirit's goal is to cut off the voice of the Lord, stop the war cry of the saints, and to remove the presence of God from your midst. In Joshua 10:16 (NASB), "Now these five kings had fled and hidden themselves in the cave at Makkedah." Makkedah, which in the Hebrew language means a place of shepherds. The enemy will hide to keep from being discovered while leading God's people astray through false deception. He has darkened the understanding of the truth concerning the Word of God. Colossians 2:8 NASB tells us, "See to it that no one takes you captive through philosophy and empty deception, according to the tradition of men, according to the elementary principles of the world, rather than according to Christ."

Don't Give the Devil a Foothold in Your Life

The greatest work that God is doing in you is being done in a region of darkness. God has to keep you hidden and make it look like you are not going to make it out. But everything the enemy tried to do, God has it written in His book. Acts 26:16–18 (NASB) instructs us:

> "But arise and stand on your feet; for this purpose I have appeared to you, to appoint you a minister and a witness not only to the things which you have seen, but also to the things in which I will appear to you; delivering you from the Jewish people and from the Gentiles, to whom I am sending you, to open their eyes so that they may turn from darkness to light and from the dominion of Satan to God, in order that they may receive forgiveness of sins and an inheritance among those who have been sanctified by faith in Me."

Guide your feet into the way of peace. Jesus is light, and he who follows Him will not walk in darkness. We must learn to discern between the spiritual struggles of the invisible works of hell behind the scenes and the humanistic behavior of individuals. God has called us to spiritual warfare prayers that will drive evil forces back so the will of God can advance.

Paul admonishes us: Ephesians 6:18 (NASB) "Put on the full armor of God, that you may be able to stand firm against the schemes of the devil." This military stance is not directed against you, but against the devil and his high level of demonic powers. We not only face the devil, but we must also contend with his schemes, deceit, and craftiness. The apostle Paul is warning us that the devil's entire system of warfare against us is based on deception. He fights us with sudden assault and cunning onslaught. Don't give the enemy an opportunity to take control of your emotions today because a foothold allows Satan to invade and take over other areas of your life.

Satan isn't trying to liberate you, he wants to establish a foothold in your life. John 10:10 confirms this: "The thief comes only to steal, and kill, and destroy; I came that they might have life, and might have it abundantly." Once he gets into an area of sin, he will make it harder for you to turn back to God. First Peter 5:8 (NASB) warns us: "Be of sober spirit, be on the alert. Your adversary, the devil prowls about like a roaring lion, seeking someone to devour." Being sober means you deny the enemy access.

Pull yourself together, "Therefore, gird your minds for action, keep sober in spirit, fix your hope completely on the grace to be brought to you at the revelation of Jesus Christ" (1 Pet.1:13 NASB). Alertness is required because our enemy rarely shows himself for who he is. He almost always masks himself as a religious personality, almost always endeavoring somehow in some way to be alert to approach you subtly so that you can't recognize the reality of who he is.

How does Satan get a foothold in your life? Through negative emotions, guilt, or shame. But when you believe the truth through the work of the Holy Spirit; Paul gives us a good reason to build on truth, so it tears down the lies of Satan. Philippians 4:8 (NASB) admonishes us: "Finally, brethren, whatever is true, whatever is honorable, whatever is right, whatever is pure, whatever is lovely, whatever is of good repute, if there is any excellence and if anything worthy of praise, let your mind dwell on these things."

PART III

The Assignment
(Approval)

"For whatever was written in earlier times was written for our instruction, so that through perseverance and the encouragement of the Scriptures we might have hope."
— Romans 15:14 (NASB)

CHAPTER 13

SPIRITUAL AWAKENING

There is a spiritual awakening that is about to hit the body of Christ. A spiritual awakening is a committed focus that builds a foundation for agreement that brings spiritual breakthrough over cities and regions. This occurs when our eyes are opened through a fresh revelation of the greatness of God, leading to an inward hunger to seek and follow and experience more of God. It is a spirit of wisdom and revelation in the knowledge of Him. The word wisdom is used to describe insight or wisdom not naturally attained. In other words, this is not natural human wisdom; this is special insight.

The word revelation refers to something that has been revealed or hidden for a long time and then suddenly, almost instantaneously, becomes clear and visible to the mind or eye.

Revelation knowledge is something that has been there all along but was not evident to you until the curtain or veil have been pulled back. This is critical for advancing the kingdom of God in our communities and cities. Why? Because many have fallen asleep spiritually (consciously). Their spiritual senses have become dull and cold to things of God. First Thessalonians 5:6 (NASB) declares, "So then let us not sleep as others do, but let us be alert and sober."

God is awakening our consciences, the inner sense of what is right or wrong in one's conduct or motives, impelling one toward right action. The word conscience is derived from the Latin word conscientia, meaning privity of knowledge or with knowledge. A lot of people have heard about Jesus but do not know Him.

Two Important Principles of the Apostolic/ Prophetic Ministry

1. Evangelism is sharing what we know about Christ Jesus for the purpose of leading others into a personal relationship with Him. In John 15:5 (NASB), Jesus says, "I am the vine, you are the branches; he who abides in Me, and I in Him, he bears much fruit; for apart from Me you can do nothing."

The word abides simply means to remain. People with genuine faith will submit to Christ's authority over their lives. They won't deny or abandon Christ's truth.

Jesus gives a command to His disciples that carries down to our generation. "And He said to them, Go into all the world and preach the gospel to all creation" (Mark 16:15 NASB). It's important that we receive the renewed, regenerated heart. It will cause you to walk in the will of God, carefully observing His commandment and ordinances.

2. Discipleship is training that makes people more willing to obey God, with the ability to control themselves of bad behaviors. John 8:31-32 (NASB) says, "Jesus therefore was saying to those Jews who had believed Him, "If you abide in My word, then you are truly disciples of Mine; and you will know the truth, and the truth shall make you free."

Let's look at evangelism according to the Parable of the Sower in which scattered seeds had fallen on four different types of soils (Luke 8:9–15 NASB).

A man's reception of God's Word is determined by the condition of his heart:

1. Hard ground represents someone who is hardened by sin; he hears but does not understand the Word, and Satan plucks the message away, keeping the heart dull and preventing the Word from making an impact.

2. Stony ground represents a person who professes the Word; however, his heart is not changed, and when trouble arises, his so-called faith quickly disappears.

3. Thorny ground represents one who seems to receive the Word but whose heart is full of riches, pleasures, and lusts; the things of

this world take his time and attention away from the Word, and he ends up having no time for it.

4. Good ground represents the one who hears, understands, and receives the Word, and then allows the Word to accomplish its results in his life.

The Breaker Anointing

A breaker anointing is God's power to press through and break every hindrance and opposition that's blocking our supernatural breakthrough. Micah 2:13 (NASB) tells us, "The breaker goes up before them; they break out, pass through the gate, and go out by it. So their King goes on before them, and the Lord at their head."

What are we breaking from? Isaiah 49:19 (NASB) says: "For your waste and desolate places, and your destroyed land. Surely now you will be too cramped for the inhabitants, and those who swallowed you will be far away." The breaker anointing purpose is to remove hindrances, roadblocks, obstacles, and limitations. Anything that's blocking the presence of God from entering a region. This anointing will cause ministries to explode with resurrection power to advance the Gospel of Jesus Christ. You can expect a new level of ministry, signs, wonders, healings, deliverance, miracles, finances, and revelations.

One of the oils of this season is called spikenard which is a costly, trustworthy, and genuine oil. It was used by Mary, the sister of Lazarus, to anoint the Lord Jesus Christ, as she poured out her heart at His feet. John 12:3 (NASB) declares: "Mary therefore took a pound of very costly perfume of pure nard, and anointed the feet of Jesus, and wiped His feet with her hair; and the house was filled with the fragrance of the perfume." Mary gave Jesus something that was so precious to her, sacrificial worship. It was pure intimate devotion and extravagant worship, without regard to the cost. As a result of Mary's devotion to Jesus, the house was filled with aroma.

The anointing destroys the yoke, breaks the cord off of our necks, sets the captives free, and removes the hindrances. The breaker anointing is the core anointing of the apostolic church for advancement. It pierces and causes sudden breakthroughs.

Isaiah 45:8 (NASB) says, "Drip down, O heavens, from above, and let the clouds pour down righteousness; let the earth open up and salvation bear fruit, and righteousness spring up with it. I, the Lord, have created it." This type of anointing will break through the natural atmosphere and literally usher in the glory of God. It shakes every shackle loose, demonic forces and released the power of God to believe the impossible. It takes a breaker anointing to impact and transform the spiritual atmosphere in your city or region.

We will see the glory of the Lord show up suddenly, lifting restrictions to the move of God. His explosive power will produce revivals of deliverance and healing in the land.

"He that dwelleth in the secret place of the most High shall abide under the shadow of the Almighty" (Ps. 91:1 KJV). The word dwelleth means to live in or at a specified place.

Where? The secret place, a hiding place where God will shield you. The blessings promised here are not for all believers, but for those who live in close fellowship with God.

Warriors sharpen your arrows (the Word of God).

> "For the word of God is living and active and full of power and sharper than any two-edged sword, and piercing as far as the division of the soul and spirit, of both joints and marrow, and able to judge the thoughts and intentions of the heart" (Heb. 4:12 NASB).

An arrow is a symbol of energy, precision, and accuracy, that which helps one go to depths of a matter or situation. God gives knowledge, wisdom, and understanding to the wise. "It is He who reveals the profound and hidden things; He knows what is in the darkness, and the light dwells with Him" (Dan. 2:22 NASB).

You have the power to change your destiny by filling your heart with the Word of God. Because what comes out of it will produce death or life.

God has given us a mandate to go and prepare the body of Christ. We are the hidden warriors who have been waiting for the timing of God's manifestation. God had reserved us for such a time as this. Isaiah 42:9 (NASB) tells us: "Behold, the former things have come to pass, now I declare new things; before they spring forth I proclaim them to you." It's already stirring. Anyone that has an ear, should pay close attention to what the Lord is speaking.

He is stirring us out of our complacency. He is releasing a fresh anointing of His Spirit upon us. He is releasing sudden surprises and supernatural supplies. The prophetic explosion has opened the windows of heaven. He is restoring everything you lost.

"Now faith is the assurance of the things hope for, the conviction of things not seen" (Heb. 11:1 NASB). Recognize that your faith will grow only as much as you feed on God's Word. "So faith comes from hearing and hearing by the word of Christ" (Rom. 10:17 NASB). Build your faith upon His Word.

Matthew 17:20 (NLT) informs us: "You don't have enough faith, Jesus told them. I tell you the truth, if you had faith even as small as a mustard seed, you could say to this mountain, move from here to there, and it would move. Nothing would be impossible." "The effective prayer of a righteous man can accomplish much" (James 5:16 NASB). The word effective means successful in producing a desired or intended result.

First John 5:14–15 (NASB) states:

> "And this is the confidence which we have before
> Him, that, if we ask anything according to His

will, He hears us. And if we know that He hears
us in whatever we ask, we know that we have the
requests which we have asked from Him."

Do you want your prayers to be more powerful? Pray the
Scriptures for they will increase your faith. And you're taking the
situation out of your hands, and releasing it to God. Jeremiah
42:3 (NASB) says: "That the LORD your God may tell us the
way in which we should walk and the thing that we should do."
By praying His Word, you will see His results. Commit to praying
the Scriptures aloud daily.

The Power of God's Word

Every believer, who is called to be an ambassadorship to the
kingdom of God, must proclaim the Word of God. Second
Corinthians 5:20 (NASB) admonishes us: "Therefore, we are
ambassadors for Christ, as though God were entreating through
us; we beg you on behalf of Christ, be reconciled to God." We are
responsible to carry out the revealed truth. Deuteronomy 29:29
(KJV) inspires us: "The secret things belong unto the LORD our
God: but those things which are revealed belong unto us and to
our children for ever, that we may do all the words of this law."

Paul tells us that God is the divine author of all Scriptures in 2
Timothy 3:16-17 (NASB): "All Scripture is inspired by God and
profitable for teaching, for reproof, for correction, for training in
righteousness; that the man of God may be adequate, equipped

for every good work." The Word of God to all believers are life, godliness, and rewards.

The Bible contains the mind of God, the state of man, the way of salvation, and the path for righteous living. There are no circumstances you will ever face where the Word of God will not have something to say and pray for. Why? God says in Jeremiah 1:12 (NASB), "You have seen well, for I am watching over My word to perform it." The book of Second Timothy teaches us how to live, serve, and persevere successfully in perilous times.

Paul's message to Timothy and us is that what the Lord requires in His workers, Second Timothy 4:2-4 (NASB) tells us: "Preach the word; be ready in season and out of season; reprove, rebuke, exhort, with great patience and instruction. For the time will come when they will not endure sound doctrine; but wanting to have their ears tickled, they will accumulate for themselves teachers in accordance to their own desires; and will turn away their ears from the truth, and will turn aside to myths."

Apostle Paul began this verse with "For I am" which revealed his eagerness and excitement to spread the good news of the gospel. In Romans, he wrote, "For I am not ashamed of the gospel, for it is the power of God for salvation to everyone who believes, to the Jew first and also to the Greek" (Rom. 1:16 NASB). The gospel changes people, it delivers them, it frees them, and it heals them. The gospel brings people into the fullness of what God intended them to be.

Paul didn't want Christians to be ignorant of certain truths about the things of the Spirit. Spiritual gifts are a God given ability to serve the church effectively. They are divine enablements for ministry, given by the Holy Spirit in some measure to all believers and are to be completely under His control and to be used for the building up of the Body of Christ, all to the glory of God through Jesus Christ.

A spiritual gift is not the same as a natural talent. Spiritual gifts are given to benefit mankind and the church in the realm of the Spirit, the realm of an individual's relationship to God. Talents deal more with the surfaces of life. Only Christians have spiritual gifts because these gifts are given only to those in whom the Spirit of Christ has come to dwell, as First Corinthians 12:7 (NASB) tells us, "But to each one is given the manifestation of the Spirit for the common good."

You must hide the Word of God in your heart. Ephesians 4:14 (NASB) assures us here:

> "As a result, we are no longer to be children, tossed here and there by waves, and carried about by every wind of doctrine, by the trickery of men, by craftiness in deceitful scheming." A solid foundation in the Word brings spiritual stability.

Let the Word of God divinely set order in His house as He teaches and trains us in spiritual truth.

"And God has appointed some in the church, first apostles, second prophets, third teachers, then miracles, then gifts of healing, helps, administrators, various kinds of tongues" 1 Corinthians 12:28 (NASB).

CHAPTER 14

GOD'S GIFT UNTO THE CHURCH

The Gifts of the Spirit are special endowments of supernatural power of God influenced by the Holy Spirit.

"Now there are varieties of gifts, but the same Spirit. And there are varieties of ministries, and the same Lord. And there are varieties of effects, but the same God who works all things in all persons. But to each one is given the manifestation of the Spirit for the common good. For to one is given the word of wisdom through the Spirit, and to another the word of knowledge according to the same Spirit; to another faith by the same Spirit, to another gifts of healing by the one Spirit, and to another the effecting of miracles, and to another prophecy, and to another the distinguishing of spirits, to another various kinds of tongues, and to another the interpretation tongues. But one and the same Spirit works all these things, distributing to each one individually just as He wills" (1 Cor. 12:4-12 NASB).

These gifts are divided into three sections, revelation, power, and inspiration. First John 5:7-8 (NASB) states, "And it is the Spirit who bears witness, because the Spirit is the truth. For there are three that bear witnesses, the Spirit and the water and the blood; and the three are in agreement."

1. Revelation Gifts—God is revealing His truth to man. The word of wisdom is revealing a prophetic future under the anointing of God and revealing a fact that is already in existence with a divine purpose. It cannot be seen or heard naturally, and the word of knowledge is the revelation of a fact that exists, past or present. The discerning of spirits has three areas in which this gift operates: the divine, the demonic, and the human or natural. This gift is used to discern the devil, not any human spirit.

2. Power Gifts—God imparts His own divine power and ability to man. The gift of faith is a special faith that supernaturally achieves what is impossible through human instruments. The gift of healing is when God, through the power of the Holy Spirit, performs supernatural exploits that cannot be humanly explained. The working of miracles is the supernatural demonstration of the power of God enabling the believer to accomplish something which by the laws of nature would be impossible.

3. Inspiration Gifts—God brings His anointing and blessings unto the church. The gift of prophecy is the anointed speaking

forth of words of edification, exhortation, and comfort, and are supernaturally given unto the church. The gift

of tongues is the ministry of proclaiming, in a public meeting, a message from God in a language not understood by the person giving it. Interpretation of tongues is when a message in tongues has been given to interpret what was said.

These gifts have to do with corporate worship, not personal worship. First Corinthians 14:3 (NASB) says, "But one who prophesies speaks to men for edification and exhortation and consolation."

The Power of the Anointing

When Jesus ascended into heaven, He anointed us with the Holy Spirit and power. He wants us to do the same things that He did on the earth and even greater things. John 14:12 (NASB) says, "Truly, truly, I say to you, he who believes in Me, the works that I do shall he do also; and greater works than these shall he do; because I go to the Father."

> "The Spirit of the Lord is upon Me, because He anointed Me to preach the gospel to the poor. He has sent Me to proclaim release to the captives, and recovery of sight to the blind, to set free those who are downtrodden, to proclaim the favorable year of the Lord" (Luke 4:18-19 NASB).

It is God who confirms, consecrated and anoint us with the gifts of the Holy Spirit. The anointing empowers us to boldly and fearlessly tell others about Jesus. The anointing enables us to perform mighty signs, wonders, and miracles. Mark 16:19-20 (NKJV) says,

> "So then, after the Lord had spoken to them, He was received up into heaven, and sat down at the right hand of God. And they went out and preached everywhere, the Lord working with them and confirming the word through the accompanying signs."

The anointing has the power to destroy every yoke and remove every burden in our lives. Isaiah 10:27 (NASB) predicts, "So it will be in that day, that his burden will be removed from your shoulders and his yoke from your neck, and the yoke will be broken because of fatness."

The anointing will enable us to reap in a massive end-time harvest of souls. It is the will of God to bring the multitudes to repentance. Romans 2:4 (NASB) says,

> "Or do you think lightly of the riches of His kindness and forbearance and patience, not knowing that the kindness of God leads you to repentance?"

If we yield to the Holy Spirit, and plug into His powerful anointing, God will use us mightily. Think about the battery life of the computer being unplugged; life goes out of it. You will not be able to get on until it is plugged in and charged up.

The same thing happens when you become unplugged from your power source— the Holy Spirit. These are ways to get plugged into the power of the Holy Spirit. Saturate yourself with the Word of God, believe what the Word of God says, pray earnestly, fast, and submit to the Holy Spirit.

Paul did not present the Gospel with persuasive words; it was backed by demonstration of undeniable power. First Corinthians 4:20 (NASB) informs us, "For the kingdom of God does not consist in words, but in power." The anointing produces power and conviction. Acts 10:38 (NASB) says, "You know of Jesus of Nazareth, how God anointed Him with the Holy Spirit and with power, and how He went about doing good, and healing all who were oppressed by the devil; for God was with Him."

First John 2:27 (NASB) states:

> "And as for you, the anointing which you received
> from Him abides in you, and you have no need for
> anyone to teach you; but as His anointing teaches
> you about all things, and is true and is not a lie,
> and just as it has taught you, you abide in Him."

We need to know the role of the Holy Spirit as we speak God's secret wisdom, which was wisdom hidden from human understanding. Because this world cannot perceive, recognize or understand the glory of the Lord.

> "But as it is written, Eye hath not seen, nor ear heard, neither have entered into the heart of man, the things which God hath prepared for them that love him. But God hath revealed them unto us by his Spirit: for the Spirit searcheth all things, yea, the deep things of God. For what man knoweth the things of a man, save the spirit of man which is in him? even so the things of God knoweth no man, but the Spirit of God" (1 Cor. 2:9-11 KJV).

Without the Holy Spirit enabling us to examine and discern clearly what God is saying, ministering the Word of God would be impossible.

The Good Fight of Faith

Faith is we believe that God's words are faithful, constant, and reliable. If we are going to invade and occupy the territory of our assignment, we must be willing to fight. First Timothy 6:12 (NASB) tells us: "Fight the good fight of faith; take hold of the eternal life to which you were called, and you made the good confession in the presence of many witnesses."

Submission means to submit, surrender, and obey the Word of God, which simply means to yield your will to God's will.

Obedience means that you turn your resignation in to God and allow Him to begin to work in you His purpose, plan, and destiny.

Just throw your hands up in submission. Fighting to win demands submission to God and resisting the devil. Fighting can be as simple as "walking by faith and not by sight" (2 Cor. 5:7 (NASB). Faith means to totally rely on God and walk in the stability of His Word, by standing firm in what it says. James 4:7 (KJV) tells us, "Submit yourselves therefore to God. Resist the devil, and He will flee from you." James 5:16 (KJV) also tells us, "the effective fervent prayers of a righteous man avails much."

When you meet spiritual resistance when you pray, continue to press through. This will build strength in your inner being as you press in, contend, resist, and fight.

The Apostle Paul didn't teach the church at Ephesus principles of spiritual warfare for nothing. He knew how intense the wrestling match with principalities and powers would be. It takes a unified apostolic body of believers to learn quickly how to influence a territory. In Deuteronomy 32:30a (NASB) it asks, "How could one chase a thousand, and two put ten thousand to flight". Being one with God equals a whole army. We cannot afford to ignore the spiritual opposition in our daily lives. We must be battle ready; "And let us not be weary in well doing: for in due season, we shall reap, if we faint not" (Gal. 6:9 KJV).

Stand in faith and get your spoils back. The enemy hope that his pressure will outlast you. Outlasting the enemy means fighting the good fight of faith and enduring until the end.

Who Bewitched You?

Even the astrologers in King Nebuchadnezzar's court thought there is,

> "There is not a man on earth who could declare the matter for the king, inasmuch as no great king or ruler has ever asked anything like this of any magician, conjurer or Chaldean. Moreover, the thing which the king demands is difficult, and there is no one else who could declare it to the king except gods, whose dwelling place is not with mortal flesh" (Dan. 2:10-11 NASB).

Now watch, "Because of this the king became indignant and very furious, and gave orders to destroy all the wise men of Babylon. So the decree went forth that the wise men should be slain; and they looked for Daniel and his friends to kill them" (Dan. 2:12–13 NASB).

When you know whose you are and whom you serve, those who are walking contrary to the will of God, bewitching the people of God with false hope and executing the true servants, will be tested and tried. Hold your peace; you don't need to defend the calling and anointing upon your life.

Seek God for godly wisdom, knowledge, and understanding. Daniel urged His friends to ask the God of heaven to show them His mercy by telling them the secret, so they would not be executed along with the other wise men of Babylon. And God answered Daniel that night in a vision.

While people are trying to execute your character and integrity, get into the presence of the almighty God and let Him reveal to them who you are. In this season, stay focused on your God given assignment, and don't allow the opinions of others to move you. You fought too hard and have been through too many storms, spiritual warfare, and attacks to let those win, who don't have a clue who God has anointed you to become.

You are a servant of the Most High God, so give Him praise and glory for sustaining you. Become a giant slayer like David. In First Samuel 17:45 (NASB), he said, "You come to me with a sword, a spear, and a javelin, but I come to you in the name of the Lord of hosts, the God of the armies of Israel, whom you have taunted."

The most important lesson to learn from David on how to fight our giants is that the battle is the Lord's. There are three words that are so important to remember when God has chosen you to become a giant slayer: trust, faith, and victory. "For the weapons of our warfare are not of the flesh, but divinely powerful for the destruction of fortresses" (2 Cor. 10:4 NASB).

CHAPTER 15

SPIRITUAL WARFARE

The information about how to disarm satanic power is in Luke 11:20–22 (NASB):

> "But if I cast out demons by the finger of God, then the kingdom of God has come upon you. When a strong man, fully armed, guards his own homestead, his possessions are undisturbed; but when someone stronger than he attacks him and overpowers him, he takes away from him all his armor on which he had relied, and distributes his plunder."

If we want church growth, we have to build a powerful prayer base. There are three levels of spiritual warfare: the ground level involves casting demons out of individuals; the occult level involves more organized "powers of darkness"; and the strategic level directly confronts territorial spirits assigned by Satan to coordinate activities over a geographic area.

Satan has the ability to control the hearts and minds of unbelievers. His desire is to keep them blinded and ignorant to the truth of God's words. His main focus is to keep your emotions in false hope, without the saving knowledge of Christ. Satan has organized forces to help him in the war, found in Ephesians 6:12 (NKJV), "For we do not wrestle against flesh and blood, but against principalities, against powers, against the rulers of the darkness of this age, against spiritual hosts of wickedness in the heavenly places."

God has given us armor and weapons as seen in Ephesians 6:13-18 (NKJV):

> "Therefore, take up the whole armor of God, that you may be able to withstand in the evil day, and having done all, to stand. Stand therefore, having girded your waist with truth, having put on the breastplate of righteousness, and having shod your feet with the preparation of the gospel of peace; above all, taking the shield of faith with which you will be able to quench all the fiery darts of the wicked one. And take the helmet of salvation, and the sword of the Spirit, which is the word of God; praying always with all prayer and supplication in the Spirit, being watchful to this end with all perseverance and supplication for all the saints. Be devoted to prayer and to the ministry of the word."

Five demonic spirits will attack the apostolic/prophetic move of God. Put your feet on the neck of the enemy.

1. Spirit of Jezebel—this demonic spirit leads to injustice, fear, poverty, confusion, and defeat.

2. Spirit of Python and Cobra—this demonic spirit causes an inability to move forward in the things of God and will always resist spiritual warfare.

3. Spirit of Sabotage—this demonic spirit darkens your spiritual understanding, bringing a lack of joy and a feeling of bondage.

4. Spirit of Goliath—this demonic spirit lead to barrenness and isolation. It wants to keep you unbridled and too proud to submit to true spiritual authority so that you will be isolated.

5. Spirit of Opposition—this demonic spirit seeks to get you to attack others' reputation, to bring discredit to leaders, and to stop true prophetic revelation from going forth or to release false prophets.

The goal of these demonic spirits is to cut off the voice of the Lord, to stop the war cry of the saints, and to remove the presence of God from your midst. Second Corinthians 10:4 (NKJV) tells us, "For the weapons of our warfare are not carnal but mighty in God for pulling down strongholds."

Some of these strongholds are easily identifiable. Others require scriptural testing and trying of the spirit. Discerning of the spirit, the supernatural gift given by the Holy Spirit, enables believers to determine, not only demonic spirits, but human spirits. We need an understanding of the spiritual realm to properly and effectively wage an overcoming war.

> "Beloved, do not believe every spirit, but test the spirits to see whether they are from God; because many false prophets have gone out into the world. By this you know the Spirit of God: every spirit that confesses that Jesus Christ has come in the flesh is from God" (1 John 4:1–2 NASB).

We must keep our lives shielded through the blood of Jesus Christ. We have protection through the Word, the name of Jesus, and the blood of Jesus against all the power of the enemy. "Behold, I have given you authority to tread upon serpents and scorpions, and over all the power of the enemy, and nothing shall injure you" (Luke 10:19 NASB).

Our spiritual warfare is against principalities. Ephesians 6:12 (NKJV) confirms this:

> "For we do not wrestle against flesh and blood, but against principalities, against powers, against the rulers of the darkness of this age, against spiritual hosts of wickedness in the heavenly places."

Principalities are ruling demon spirits, possessing executive authority or governmental rule in the world. They oppose the truth of God. It is an organization of demons. In Matthew 12:24 (NASB) says: "But when the Pharisees heard it, they said, "This man casts out demons only by Beelzebul the ruler of the demons. The devil is called "Beelzebub," meaning lord of the dwelling, in which these wicked spirits are subject to and operate under Satan's dominion. They, like their chief prince, direct, control, rule and carry out the present darkness of this world. Principalities are also defined as a territory ruled by a prince, the position, authority, or jurisdiction of a prince; i.e., sovereignty.

It is Satan's purpose to deceive and keep people in a territory from obtaining the knowledge of God's truth and salvation through His Son Jesus Christ. The Greek word for "deceive" is planao, which means to "cause to roam from safety, truth or virtue, go astray, seduce, wander, fall away from the truth, and to be out of the way.

Satan's major success, in deceiving a nation, is due to the lack of discernment on the part of the people. The people are blind to the invisible forces of supernatural evil that are operating and influencing their visible human agents.

Strategic Prayer Strategy

Believers are a people who are at war. Ephesians 6:12 (NASB) says,

> "For our struggle is not against flesh and blood, but against the rulers, against the powers, against the world forces of this darkness, against the spiritual forces of wickedness in the heavenly places."

The war is spiritual, and according to Ephesians 6, it is against the forces of evil spirits and not any human person.

The Lord Jesus Christ has given us delegated power and authority to trample the enemy and the legal right to use His name. We must possess the kingdom of God on the earth by force. "The kingdom of heaven suffers violence, and violent men take it by force" (Matt. 11:12 NASB). We are the Lord's instrument of war as He says in Jeremiah 51:20 (NASB), "You are My war-club, My weapon of war; and with you I shatter nations, and with you I destroy kingdoms."

The Holy Spirit will, upon your continual yielding to His will over time, lead you into developing your own style of scriptural warfare to bring glory and edification to the church. Like most aspects of your spiritual growth, it is a process gained "So the word of the Lord to them will be, order on order, order on order, line on line, line on line, a little here, a little there, that they may go and stumble backward, be broken, snared, and taken captive" (Isa. 28:13 NASB).

God honors the intent of the heart, and you will see Him respond to your faith. As you grow in your knowledge and vocabulary in spiritual warfare, let the Holy Spirit lead you in the nature of words during your prayer time. Be sensitive to the leading of the Holy Spirit in showing you what to say.

Spiritual warfare prayer, as with all prayer is empowered by our faith in Christ through the delegated authority in which He gives to every believer through His shed blood and His victory over Satan and through His work of the Cross on our behalf. Believers must understand their position in Christ, that they are joined to His Spirit, First Corinthians 6:17 (NASB) tells us: "But the one who joins himself to the Lord is one spirit with Him."

The born-again, spirit-filled believer functions through His position in Christ. The believer must, therefore, know who he or she is in Christ and the power that has been delegated to them by the Holy Spirit.

The Believer "walks by faith, not by sight" (2 Cor. 5:7 NASB). Therefore, the weapons of spiritual warfare must be known, recognized, understood, and appropriated, that is, taken possession of. Your mind and heart must be directed to the Father, asking in Jesus's name, or to Jesus, Himself, asking in His name. Before you pray, yield to the Holy Spirit in Jesus's name and ask His Spirit of prayer to fall upon you and to lead you with faith-filled words. Back your prayers with faith (trust in Christ). Faith moves God's heart and hand to act on your behalf.

Faith must be unwavering, determined, and steadfast. Speak your prayers aloud into the atmosphere to nullify the devil's power. He is the prince of the power of the air. The word of God, spoken in faith, has supernatural power to accomplish His desires and purposes. Isaiah 55:10-11 (NASB) confirms this: "For as the rain and the snow come down from heaven, and do not return there without watering the earth, and making it bear and sprout, and furnishing seed to the sower and bread to the eater; so shall My word be which goes forth from My mouth; It shall not return to Me empty, without accomplishing what I desire, and without succeeding in the matter for which I sent it."

Praying through means praying with persistence until you receive and see the result. Rom. 8:26-27 (NASB) informs us:

> "And in the same way the Spirit also helps our weakness; for we do not know how to pray as we should, but the Spirit Himself intercedes for us with groanings too deep for words; and He who searches the hearts knows what the mind of the Spirit is, because He intercedes for the saints according to the will of God."

When you don't know what to prayer for, always pray in tongues. The Holy Spirit will pray according to the will of God.

CHAPTER 16

THE MINISTRY OF THE INTERCESSOR

Intercession isn't for the zealous few; it's a calling and destiny of the chosen ones. It's a divine appointment. John 15:16 (NASB) speaks of the calling, "You did not choose Me, but I chose you, and appointed you, that you would go and bear fruit, and that your fruit should remain, that whatever you ask of the Father in My name, He may give to you." You are chosen.

An intercessor makes themself no reputation. They must take on the form of a servant, humble themselves and become obedient. Joshua 1:8 (NASB) exhorts:

> "This book of the law shall not depart from your mouth, but you shall meditate on it day and night, so that you may be careful to do according to all that is written in it; for then you will make your way prosperous, and then you will have success."

Why? Because you are called to stand in between heaven and Earth, standing in the gap and interceding and praying for others. Intercessors pray for godly wisdom. James 1:5 (NASB) says, "But if any of you lacks wisdom, let him ask of the God, who gives to all men generously and without reproach, and it will be given to him."

The ministry of the intercessor will flow from these gifts: exhortation, giving, word of knowledge, word of wisdom, discerning of spirits, and tongues and interpretation.

> "Devote yourselves to prayer, keeping alert in it with an attitude of thanksgiving; praying at the same time for us as well, that God will open up to us a door for the word, so that we may speak forth the mystery of Christ, for which I have also been imprisoned" (Col. 4:2-3 NASB).

James 5:16–17 (NASB) says, "Therefore, confess your sins to one another, and pray for one another so that you may be healed. The effective prayer of a righteous man can accomplish much. Elijah was a man with a nature like ours, and he prayed earnestly that it would not rain, and it did not rain on the earth for three years and six months."

Intercession is not a matter of saying the right words but of having the right heart. If we love the Lord with all our heart, we have the right heart. Deuteronomy 6:5 (NASB) says, "You shall love the Lord your God with all your heart and with all your soul and with all your might."

Intercessors are not ignorant of the devil's devices because they have been gifted to see beyond the natural and into the spiritual. Ephesians 6:12 (NASB) says, "For our struggle is not against flesh and blood, but against the rulers, against the powers, against the world forces of this darkness, against the spiritual forces of wickedness in the heavenly places."

The ministry of intercessor is a divine appointment. The Bible expresses the very nature of this ministry; the great heaviness of spirit and burden of prayer experienced by those in intercession. Lamentations 3:48-50 (NASB) tells us, "My eyes run down with streams of water because of the destruction of the daughter of my people. My eyes pour down unceasingly, without stopping. Until the Lord looks down and sees from heaven."

When God speaks of intercessors and their persistence in prayer, He says that they should not rest until they have prepared a way for the people to return back to repentance. Lamentations 2:18-19 (NASB) informs us:

> "Their heart cried out to the Lord, O wall of the daughter of Zion, let your tears run down like a river day and night; give yourself no relief; let your eyes have no rest. Arise, cry aloud in the night, at the beginning of the night watches; pour out your heart like water, before the presence of the Lord; lift up your hands to Him for the life of your little ones who are faint because of hunger at the head of every street."

As an intercessor you must grow spiritually; you cannot remain a babe in Christ and be an intercessor. God has given you a job, an assignment, in Him. As an intercessor, you need to have all three of these qualities in operation:

(1) Wisdom is the ability to discern or judge what is true and right. (Proverbs 4:7 NASB "The beginning of wisdom is: Acquire wisdom; and with all your acquiring, get understanding").

(2) Knowledge is the state or fact of knowing what has been perceived, discovered or learned. (Proverbs 2:10 NASB "For wisdom will enter your heart, and knowledge will be pleasant to your soul").

(3) Understanding is the quality or condition of one who understands, comprehend and having good sense of discernment. (Proverbs 2:6 NASB "For the Lord gives wisdom; from His come knowledge and understanding").

You must open your ears and hear what He is saying because the Scripture says:

> "But as it is written, Eye hath not seen, nor ear heard, neither have entered into the heart of man, the things which God hath prepared for them that love him" (1 Cor. 2:9 KJV).

The ministry of the intercessor is a divine appointment as explained here in Isiah:

> "On your walls, O Jerusalem, I have appointed watchmen; all day and all night they will never keep silent. You who remind the Lord, take no rest for yourselves; and give Him no rest until He establishes and makes Jerusalem a praise in the earth" (Isa. 62:6-7 NASB).

The intercessor must have the mind of Christ, "Have this same attitude in yourselves which was also in Christ Jesus" (Phil. 2:5 NASB). To have the mind of Christ means that we don't think and operate the way we did in former times. Isaiah 11:2 (NASB) says, "And the Spirit of the Lord will rest on Him, the Spirit of wisdom and understanding, the Spirit of counsel and strength, the Spirit of knowledge and of the fear of the Lord." In order to have the mind of Christ, we are going to have to present ourselves to God for a transforming of our carnal minds. God, by His mind operating fully in us, can penetrate deep within the hidden chambers of our souls and not only expose, cleanse, and heal these areas, but also root out the strongholds of the enemy.

God is looking for those intercessors who will strategically stand in the gap and make the proper adjustments to bring down the strongholds of the enemy because they are the unseen warrior who fights against the wicked schemes and tactics of the enemy in the background.

CHAPTER 17

THE MINISTRY OF A WATCHMAN

A s prophetic watchmen, we must be on alert. The watchman's anointing allows us to pray against Satan's schemes and plans. It is a vital aspect of our intercession. Ephesians 6:18 (NASB) says, "With all prayer and petition pray at all times in the Spirit, and with this in view, be on the alert with all perseverance and petition for all the saints." First Peter 5:8 (NASB), in warning us about our enemy says, "Be of sober spirit, be on alert. Your adversary, the devil, prowls about like a roaring lion, seeking someone to devour." Both of these scriptures challenge us to alertness and watchfulness, not only for ourselves, but for our family and ministry. Second Corinthians 2:11 (NASB) tells us, "in order that no advantage be taken of us by Satan; for we are not ignorant of his schemes." Colossians 4:2 (NASB) exhorts, "Devote yourselves to prayer, keeping alert in it with an attitude of thanksgiving."

Be on alert; stand firm in your faith. As a watchman for the Lord, you must never keep silent. You must go through the gates of time and season. Isaiah 62:10 (NASB) encourages us: "Go through, go through the gates; clear the way for the people, build up, build up the highway."

The watchmen anointing is upon us. God is shifting us from intercessors to watchmen. Habakkuk 2:1 (KJV) tells us: "I will stand upon my watch, and set me upon the tower, and will watch to see what he will say unto me, and what I shall answer when I am reproved." God's watchmen have the ability to:

1. SEE—Isaiah 52:8 (NASB) says: "Listen! Your watchmen lift up their voices, they shout joyfully together; for they will see with their own eyes when the LORD restores Zion."

2. HEAR—Proverbs 8:32-34 (NASB) says: "Now therefore, O sons, listen to me, for blessed are they who keep my ways. Heed instruction and be wise, and do not neglect it. Blessed is the man who listens to me, watching daily at my gates, waiting at my doorposts."

3. DISCERNMENT —First John 4:1 (NASB) says: "Beloved, do not believe every spirit, but test the spirits to see whether they are from God; because many false prophets have gone out into the world."

The watchman needs these three weapon in their arsenal: the Bible, a commentary, and a concordance.

The watchman has God's anointing of discerning Satan's strategies to hinder and attack. Ezekiel 33:1-3 (NASB) tells us about the duty of a watchman: "And the word of the LORD came to saying, 'Son of man, speak to the sons of your people, and say to them, if I bring a sword upon a land, and the people of the land take one man from among them and make him their watchman; and he sees the sword coming upon the land, and he blows on the trumpet and warns the people."

Functions of a watchman

The primary function of a watchman is to remain focus, vigilant, and not easily distracted by the approaching danger of the enemy. The watchman is the spiritual guardian and keeper of the gates of time.

The Bible speaks of watches, which covers twenty four hours a day. Every prayer watch has a targeted goal, and understanding them will help you know what watch God has called you to. These are the eight watches of the Lord, and everyone is given a watch. Psalm 1:2 (NASB) encourages us: "But his delight is in the law of the Lord, and in His law he meditates day and night."

Eight Watches of the Lord:

1st Watch (6pm-9pm) Time to possess the gate of your day (Lam. 2:18-19; Acts 20:28).

2nd Watch (9pm-12am) Praying for the Outpouring of the Holy Spirit (Ps. 119:62; Ps. 63:5-7).

3rd Watch (12am-3am) Warfare Prayer (Judg. 7:19; Ps. 119:148).

4th Watch (3am-6am) Deliverance Prayer (Job 38:12-13; Matt. 14:22-25).

5th Watch (6am-9am) Time of Exaltation (Ex. 14:24-25; Ps. 34:15)

6th Watch (9am-12pm) Divine Protection Prayer (Ps. 91:1-16; Deut. 31:6)

7th Watch (12pm-3pm) Prosperity Release Prayer (Gen. 43:16-25; Deut. 8:18)

8th Watch (3pm-6pm) Time of Divine Direction (Acts 10:3-13; Jer. 29:11)

Every prayer watch has a purpose and understanding them will help you pray strategically.

When the watchman is in his spiritual position, he can clearly see what is happening in the church and the body of Christ, the cities, and nations, and he will be able to receive from God what the spiritual atmosphere in the heavens and in the earth is.

CHAPTER 18

TRAVAILING PRAYER

G od is calling His people back to travailing prayer. He is
searching for hearts that will intercede, and He will use them
to travail. Travailing prayer puts great compassion into your heart
for a specific purpose or person. Someone who maybe struggling
with overwhelming circumstances. Isaiah 59:16 (NASB) declares:
"And He saw that there was no man, and was astonished that there
was no one to intercede; then His own arm brought salvation to
Him; and His righteousness upheld Him."

Travailing in the Spirit means to express extreme painful labor as in
giving birth, just as a woman in the natural travails when she is about
to deliver her child. Jeremiah 22:23 (NASB) informs us: "You who
dwell in Lebanon, nested in the cedars, how you will groan when
pangs come upon you, pain like a woman in childbirth!"

Travail is a form of intense intercession given by the Holy Spirit
whereby the prayer grips the heart of God. This creates an opening
to birth the purpose and plan of God. Jeremiah 29:11 (NASB) says:

"For I know the plans that I have for you, declares the Lord, plans for welfare and not for calamity to give you a future and a hope."

The church is in the groaning position of the birth canal. If the church cries out like a barren woman longing for children, there would be a great breakthrough revival. The church has lost the art of travailing prayer. "Before she travailed, she brought forth; before her pain came, she gave birth to a boy. Who has heard such a thing? Who has seen such things? Can a land be born in one day? Can a nation be brought forth all at once? As soon as Zion travailed, she also brought forth her sons. Shall I bring to the point of birth, and not give delivery? says the Lord. Or shall I who gives delivery shut the womb? says your God" (Isa. 66:7-9 NASB). Travailing prayer has a purpose in setting the condition of the heart with His will. Travailing prayer is a deeper realm of prayer available that many believers have not known existed. Romans 8:26-27 (NASB) declares,

> "And in the same way, the Spirit also helps our weakness; for we do not know how to pray as we should, but the Spirit Himself intercedes for us with groanings too deep for words; and He who searches the hearts knows what the mind of the Spirit is, because He intercedes for the saints according to the will of God."

Just as creation groans waiting for the fullness of redemption, the Holy Spirit groans through us in prayer. He is our help, which means the Holy Spirit takes over together with us, praying against the situation we can't handle and bringing us victory. It is important for us to recognize our physical, emotional, and spiritual weaknesses. Hebrews 4:14-14 (NASB) teaches us: "Since then we a great high priest who passed through the heavens, Jesus the Son of God, let us hold fast our confession. For we do not have a high priest who cannot sympathize with our weaknesses, but One who has been tempted in all things as we are, yet without sin."

Paul points out the painful process of repentance. Because it involves a heartfelt conviction of sin, and a turning away from the sinful way of life, and turning towards God. Second Corinthians 7:10 (KJV)says, "For godly sorrow worketh repentance to salvation not to be repented of: but the sorrow of world worketh death." Worldly sorrow is unrepentant sorrow.

There is a battle going on for souls. We must be sensitive to the leading of the Holy Spirit. Because this deep passionate level of intercession affects the spiritual atmosphere, so the gospel penetrates the heart of the lost. Isaiah 66:8 (NASB) declares: "Who has heard such a thing? Who has seen such things? Can a land be born in one day? Can a nation be brought forth all at once? As soon as Zion travailed, she also brought forth her sons."

When the Word of God is sown, it will produce results. Psalm 126:5-6 (NASB) tells us: "Those who sow in tears shall reap with joyful shouting. He who goes to and fro weeping, carrying his bag of seed, shall indeed come again with a shout of joy, bringing his sheaves with him."

What is the purpose for travail? Travailing prayer gives birth to the will of God, and pulls down Satanic oppressions and barriers. Jeremiah 1:17-19 (NASB) encourages us: "Now, gird up your loins, and arise, and speak to them all which I command you. Do not be dismayed before them, lest I dismayed you before them. Now behold, I have made you today as a fortified city, and as a pillar of iron and as walls of bronze against the whole land, to the kings of Judah, to its princes, to its priests and to the people of the land. And they will fight against you, but they will not overcome you, for I am with you to deliver you, declares the LORD."

Paul expressed great emotional pain. Because the souls that he labored and birth forth was being bewitched by false teachers. Galatians 4:19 (NASB) tells us: "My children, with whom I am again in labor until Christ is formed in you." This type of travailing prayer is used when you are praying for others, whom may be facing overwhelming struggles. Now Paul had to travail in birth to bring God's power into their lives. Galatians 1:6-8 (NASB) says,

> "I am amazed that you are so quickly deserting Him
> who called you by the grace of Christ for a different
> gospel, which is really not another; only there are
> some who are disturbing you and want to distort
> the gospel of Christ. But even if we, or an angel from
> heaven, should preach to you a gospel contrary to
> what we have preached to you, he is to be accursed!
> And they had to be renewed in Christ again."

When we travail in prayer, God hears the cries of His children. Psalm 5:1-2 (NASB) inspires us: "Give ear to my words, O Lord, consider my groaning. Heed the sound of my cry for help, my King and my God, for to Thee do I pray." Travailing in prayer is a mighty spiritual weapon.

Travailing in prayer is a cry of desperation, to press in, cry out, and to passionately seek after God. The Bible tells us that Hannah poured out her heart to the Lord in First Samuel 1:10-11 (NASB): "And she, greatly distressed, prayed to the Lord and wept bitterly. And she made a vow and said, O Lord of hosts, if Thou wilt indeed look on the affliction of Thy maidservant and remember me, and not forget Thy maidservant, but wilt give Thy maidservant a son, then I will give him to the Lord all the days of his life, and a razor shall never come on his head." We too can give birth to our destiny and purpose.

What Is a Dry Atmosphere?

Air that has a low relative humility is a dry atmosphere. When the relative humility drops below about 40 percent, the air feels dry to the skin. When our praise and worship drops, it produces a dry atmosphere. The atmosphere speaks of a prevailing or surrounding influence or spirit. The atmosphere we create has a direct effect on the life and movement of the church.

Spiritual dryness can leave you emotionally drain, where you are no longer motivated by passion to serve the Lord. And it becomes a duty versus honor. Psalm 63:1 (NASB) declares: "O God, Thou art my God; I shall seek Thee earnestly; my soul thirsts for Thee, my flesh yearns for Thee, in a dry and weary land where there is no water."

Sometimes we allow our circumstances to dictate our mood. When we come to church, we are coming to worship. But if we let our problems and the situations that we are dealing with hinder our spirits, then there is no true worship. We need to learn to come to church with one thing on our minds—to worship. We need to learn to give our cares to the Lord and let Him fight our battles for us. It is hard to worship if we are fighting other battles mentally and physically. We shouldn't allow anything to hinder us in our worship and thanksgiving.

We should be expecting the Lord of glory to fill His house with His presence each and every time we gather together to lift Him up and glorify His mighty name, setting the atmosphere for the supernatural to take place. The Lord will respond to our faith when we come expecting to receive with the right attitude.

Our praise and worship doesn't move God; our faith does. Hebrews 11:6 (NASB) inspires us: "And without faith it is impossible to please Him, for he who comes to God must believe that He is, and that He is a rewarder of those who seek Him."

We must learn the importance of shifting the atmosphere; when this happens, things will change in our lives. We can truly change our atmosphere by speaking prophetic words of life.

CHAPTER 19

EXPECT THE UNEXPECTED BLESSINGS OF THE LORD

This means to be prepared for anything because something unexpected could easily happen. God released a prophetic word through Elisha, and the king's officer doubted (2 Kings 7:1-2 NASB "Then Elisha said, "Listen to the word of the Lord; thus says the Lord, 'Tomorrow about this time a measure of fine flour shall be sold for a shekel, and two measures of barley for a shekel in the gate of Samaria.' And the royal officer on whose hand the king was leaning answered the man of God and said, "Behold, if the Lord should make windows in heaven, could this thing be?" Then he said, "Behold you shall see it with your own eyes, but you shall not eat of it""). This text tells us of a famine condition that existed, and in the midst of a famine, the man of God released a word of promise from the Lord that had a set time (tomorrow, about this time). Time is the great sifter. It will challenge you how to develop great patience during your waiting season.

You have an expectation of something greater, but everything looks bad. God gave a promise through Elisha that in twenty-four hours, the economic situation in Samaria would be completely reversed. Instead of scarcity, there would be such abundance that food prices would radically drop in the city.

The king's officer doubted the prophecy, and his doubt was based on several reasons. He doubted the power of God and the creativity of God. The king's officer probably was thinking, How is this food coming to the city from above because it was surrounded by a hostile, besieging army? He had no idea that God could bring provision in a completely unexpected way.

How often does faith breaks down in this way? It knows that God is almighty and that He can do what He says. But it only sees one way and refuses to believe that such a way will be taken. The officer doubted the messenger of God. Elisha's track record of reliability should have been enough for the king's officer to believe, although the promise seemed impossible or hard to believe. The officer displayed unbelief for this new thing that could not be done. There is no way to accomplish this thing. Even if God does something good, it wouldn't be enough. Through Elisha, God pronounced a harsh judgment upon the king's doubting officer. He would see the word fulfilled but not benefit from its fulfill- ment. There is one thing I want you to see in this text, that is, while everything inside the city was getting worse and every natural evidence was defying the Word of God, outside the city gate, God was working.

Four leprous men stayed at the entrance of the gate because they were not welcome in the city. Their leprous condition made them outcasts and untouchables. God inspired those four lepers to get up from where they were and go to the Syrian camp. As they walked, God caused the Syrian army to hear a sound as great as an army marching toward them, and they fled in fear, leaving an abundant supply of food and other things behind them. The lepers understood that to remain silent and to selfishly enjoy their blessings would be a sin. They had a responsibility to share the good news.

Because of the unbelief of the king's officer, he saw others enjoy God's blessings, but he did not as he was trampled when the people rushed to get food from the camp.

Praise Is Your Defense Against Opposition

Has the Lord redeemed and done great things for you? Then, give thanks to the Lord. Those that hunger and thirst after the righteousness of the living God shall be abundantly replenished with the goodness of His house. Praise God for reconciling and restoring His favor upon you. Let the redeemed of the Lord say so. Walk in the newness of a fresh new start, leaving your old behavior and conduct.

Psalm 107:4-32 (NLT) demonstrates the power of God's love to change our lives. The Lord is gathering the wanderers (Psalm 107:4 NLT "Some wandered in the desert, lost and homeless"), prisoners (Psalm 107:10 NLT "Some sat in darkness and deepest gloom, miserable prisoners in chains"), distressed (Psalm 107:17 NLT "Some were fools in their rebellion; they suffered for their sins"), and storm-tossed (Psalm 107:23 NLT "Some went off in ships, plying the trade routes of the world"), for His purpose and glory. There is a great revival coming to the body of Christ. God knows those who are His and where to find them.

First Condition—Wanderers (v. 4-9) A wanderer is a person who have been redeemed out of the hand of the enemy but are without a dwelling place to rest their hungry and thirsty soul.

Second Condition—Prisoners (v. 10-19) A person who feels confined or trapped by a situation or set of circumstances. They are miserable and sitting in a dark place of despair. Because of this condition, they rebel against God.

Third Condition—Distressed (v. 17-20) A person suffering from body pain of anxiety, sorrow, affliction or trouble. Their appetite for the things of God are as good as gone.

Fourth Condition—Storm-tossed (v. 23–32) They are the ones who feel hopeless and overwhelmed by the repeated storms of life, as they come one after another.

God will put you in situations where you have no choice but to abandon all the trust you had in yourself and cry out to Him for deliverance. God has sent His Word to heal, deliver, and set you free. The Word of God comforts the afflicted. "Thy word is a lamp to my feet and a light to my path" (Ps. 119:105 NASB).

God is always waiting for us to cry out to Him when we are in trouble. Crying out to Him is not a sign of weakness but of strength. When you are dying spiritually, it's because you feel separated from God. Cry out. Let's come together and cry out to God, willing to repent and to obey His will and to listen to His voice as we cry out with true repentance, confessing our sins, weeping, and throwing ourselves on His altar.

When those who have been sick are restored, they must return to God with praise. Praise is our defense against opposition.

> "Then the eyes of the blind will be opened, and the ears of the deaf will be unstopped. Then the lame will leap like a deer. And the tongue of the dumb will shout for joy, for the waters will break forth in the wilderness. And streams in the Arabah" (Isa. 35:5-6 NASB).

Move Out in Faith

When you get a Word from God, and without receiving godly counsel or wisdom, you can abort the process. Because if God has spoken to you through His prophet and it's a promise from His Word, you need to stand on it until it comes to pass.

It really doesn't matter if everyone agrees with you or not. You will always find someone who says, "Well, are you sure that's what God said or is doing ?" We trust too much in fleshly wisdom rather than in the Word of God.

Waiting on God requires patience, hope rooted in faith, and expecting Him to act. Waiting for God, then means the power to do nothing. James 1:4 (NASB) says: "And let endurance have its perfect result, that you may be perfect and complete, lacking in nothing." Waiting requires endurance, according to: Hebrews 10:36 (NASB) "For you have need of endurance, so that when you have done the will of God, you may receive what was promised."

Fear grips us at the moment of decision. We become afraid and start worrying about what people are going to think if God doesn't come through. I'd rather step out, believing God for the Word to do the impossible, than never step out and never see anything happen. I would rather risk failing than never take risks at all.

CHAPTER 20

A CHANGE IS GOING TO COME

The Pharisees and their scribes began grumbling at the disciples saying, "Why do you eat and drink with the tax gathers and sinners? Jesus's reply was, "I have not come to call the righteous but sinners to repentance!" Repentance means a change of mind. They asked, "Why do the disciples of John fast often, and make prayers, and likewise the disciples of the Pharisees; but thine eat and drink?" (Luke 5:33 KJV).

Fasting and prayer is the cure for unbelief. Faith needs prayer for its development and full growth, and prayer needs fasting for the same reason. Luke 5:36-37 (NASB) tells us: "No one tears a piece from a new garment and puts it on an old garment; otherwise he will both tear the new, and the piece from the new will not match the old. And no one puts new wine into old wineskins; otherwise the new wine will burst the skins, and it will be spilled out, and the skins will be ruined." The old garment speaks of the legal system, and the new garment pictures the era of grace; they are incompatible. The fermenting action of the new wine causes pressure on the skins for which they are no longer pliable or elastic enough to bear. The skins burst, and the wine is spilled. The rituals of Judaism were too rigid to hold the joy, the exuberance, and the energy of the new dispensation (release).

Forget the former and embrace the new. Isaiah 43:18-19 (NASB) says,

> "Do not call to mind the former things or ponder the things of the past. Behold, I will do something new, now it will spring forth. Will you not be aware of it? I will even put a roadway in the wilderness, rivers in the desert."

Jesus was saying two things in Luke 5:36-37 (NASB): "No one tears a piece from a new garment and puts it on an old garment; otherwise he will both tear the new, and the piece from the new will not match the old. And no one puts new wine into old wineskins; otherwise the new wine will burst the skins, and it will be spilled out, and the skins will be ruined." He was ushering in a new life which was stronger than the old life, and He could not take His teachings and patch up the old teaching. What He is saying to us today is that there is going to be a tear in the old religion and their teachings. The followers of the old system would react violently and quickly. Why? Because "they have a form of godliness but deny the power thereof, and from such turn away" (2 Tim. 3:5 KJV). Many worship the traditions of man and not of God. The tearing and pulling apart between Jesus and the old religion was over its rituals and ceremonies. Second Corinthians 5:19-20 (NLT) tells us:

> "For God was in Christ, reconciling the world to himself, no longer counting people's sins against them. This is the wonderful message he has given us to tell others. We are Christ's ambassadors, and God is using us to speak to you. We urge you, as though Christ himself were here pleading with you. Be reconciled to God!"

Is There Order in the House?

A healthy body will function in unity and harmony. Ephesians 4:16 (NLT) tells us:

"Under his direction, the whole body is fitted together perfectly. As each part does its own special work, it helps the other parts grow, so that the whole body is healthy and growing and full of love."

There are nine purposes for the ministry of the Holy Spirit that was given unto the church after the Resurrection of Jesus Christ, as found in Ephesians 4:12–16 (NASB):

1. For the perfecting of the saints (Apostle, prophet, evangelist, pastor, teacher)

2. For the work of the ministry (This work of ministry requires work)

3. For the edifying of the body of Christ (We are to build you up to a mature man, not a baby, giving of yourself and helping others.)

4. Till we all come in the unity of the faith (This means until we live in unity without compromising our belief)

5. Of the knowledge of the Son of God (It is easy to have knowledge about so many things except Jesus. When we come into the true knowledge of the Son of God, who He is, and what He has done, and what He can do, only then we are mature.)

6. Unto a perfect man (To be perfect means mature, living in obedience to Christ, being consistent and not carried away with every new teachings that doesn't line up with the Word of God)

7. Unto the measure of the statue of the fullness of Christ (Keep your ministry active)

8. That we henceforth be no more children, tossed to and fro and carried about with every wind of doctrine, by the sleight of men (Cunning craftiness, whereby one lies in wait to deceive)

9. And to speak God's truth in love, may grow up into him in all things, which is the head, even Christ. (The ability to speak the truth in love, with a right attitude in sharing our faith with other's)

Trusting God, No Matter What

Psalm 27:14 (NASB) informs us: "Wait for the Lord; be strong, and let your heart take courage; Yes, wait for the Lord." Three Words: Wait, Hope, Expect. What does it mean to wait on God? Waiting on God is not laziness. It means readiness for any new command that may come, the ability to do nothing until the command is given. Waiting for God, then means the power to do nothing. It is a strength that holds strength in check. Waiting requires strength. It demands absolute surrender of the life to God, the confession that we are at the end of our own understanding of things, and the confession that we really do not see our way and do not know the way.

The waiting that says, "Until God shall speak, we dare not move and will not move." Lamentations 3:25 (NASB) encourages us, "The Lord is good to those who wait for Him, to the person who seeks Him."

Our attitude is important as we wait on God. Persevere in walking according to His will. Courage is to be maintained while you wait. The Bible speaks often about the importance of waiting on God. Psalm 40:1 (NASB) says, "I waited patiently for the Lord; and He inclined to me and heard my cry." Isaiah 40:31 (NASB) also speaks of waiting, "Yet those who wait for the Lord, Will gain new strength; They will mount up with wings like eagles, They will run and not get tired, They will walk and not become weary."

The Lord is good to those who wait for Him. He will, in due time, answer your prayer. Wait at His door of prayer with humility and expectancy.

Here's what happens to so many of us. We pray, weep, and cry but still have one setback, and one disappointment after another. And we begin to wonder why it is that things aren't changing. Why is it we can't get a breakthrough? Proverbs 13:12 (NASB) says, "Hope deferred makes the heart sick, but desire fulfilled is a tree of life." Wait and hope for and expect the Lord to move Be brave and of good courage. Yes, wait for and hope for and expect the Lord to return it.

The Master Key of Prayer: Abiding in Christ

Abiding in Christ and His Word abiding in us teaches us to pray in accordance with the will of God. When we abide in Christ, our self-will is kept out; the thoughts and wishes of the natural man are brought into captivity to the thoughts and wishes of Christ. Abiding in Christ renews and sanctifies the will; we ask what we will, and it is given to us. Abiding in Christ, the soul learns not only to desire, but spiritually to discern what will be for God's glory. John 15:7 (NASB) admonishes us: "If you abide in Me, and My words abide in you, ask whatever you wish, and it shall be done for you."

Abiding in Christ also involves waiting upon the Lord and entering into his peace. Psalm 62:5 (NASB) says, "My soul, wait in silence for God only, For my hope is from Him." Abiding in Christ, therefore, means to draw supernatural strength from the presence of the Lord and walk moment by moment in the leading of His Spirit.

Abiding in Christ means trusting God and making Him your refuge. Psalm 91:1-2 (NASB) assures us, "He who dwells in the shelter of the Most High will abide in the shadow of the Almighty. I will say to the Lord, "My refuge and my fortress, My God, in whom I trust!'"

The Seed of Understanding

May God give you a spirit of wisdom and revelation knowledge of Him in what He is doing. Once you get the truth, and understand it, it will motivate you in all that you do in life. "I pray that the eyes of your heart may be enlightened, so that you may know what is the hope of His calling, what are the riches of the glory of His inheritance in the saints, and what is the surpassing greatness of His power toward us who believe. These are in accordance with the working of the strength of His might" (Eph. 1:18-19 NASB).

The heart is the seat of emotions. The heart also is the seat of understanding. So, I'm praying that your spiritual eyes might be turned on. The heart is the center of the personality, and it controls the intellect, emotions, and will. It's the inner person, the seat of motives and attitudes, and the center of personality. Proverbs

23:7 (NASB) says, "For as he thinks within himself, so he is. He says to you, eat and drink! But his heart is not with you."

Jesus asked a group of scribes "Why are you thinking evil in your hearts?" (Matt. 9:4 NASB). The heart is the control center of the mind and will as well as the emotions. Paul was praying that the Ephesians church would receive a deeper spiritual understanding. There are three specific concerns that Paul had in Ephesians 1:18-19 (NASB), which he hopes the Ephesians church can understand in their walk: what the hope of His calling is; what the riches of the glory of His inheritance in the saints are; and what the surpassing greatness of His power toward us who believe is.

Now one thing we need to understand about the hope of His calling is that when you see the word hope, it's the deepest level of assuring us that what God has promised and what God is doing will come to pass.

May God open the eyes of His people so that they may turn from darkness to light and so those who have been consecrated and sanctified by faith may receive an inheritance. "But you are a chosen race, a royal priesthood, a holy nation, a people for God's own possession, that you may proclaim the excellencies of Him who has called you out of darkness into His marvelous light" (1 Pet. 2:9 NASB).

Claiming Territories for the Kingdom of God

God has called you to a specific region to tend it, water it, and care for it so they can prosper and bloom. A territory is a geographical location where one lives, works, go to school, and so forth. It is an area where someone has responsibilities with regard to a particular activity or assignment.

Demon spirits also claim territorial responsibility over a land, a family, or even individuals. These are called territorial spirits. These are spirits assigned over particular territorial locations. The behaviors or cultural patterns of people in a particular community or territory sometimes manifest the spirits controlling that community or territory.

In the days of Daniel, there was a spirit assigned over the Empire to hinder the will of God, saying:

> "But the prince of the Kingdom of Persia withstood me twenty-one days; and behold, Michael, one of the chief Princes, came to help me, for I had been left there with the kings of Persia ... then he said, Do you understand why I came to you? But I shall return to fight against the prince of Persia; so I am going forth, and behold, the prince of Greece is about to come" (Dan. 10:13, 20 NASB).

The angelic being appears to Daniel, and tells him that his prayer was heard from the first day (Dan. 10:12 NASB). But the prince of the kingdom of Persia had resisted him from bringing the message from God to Daniel. This hindering spirit was assigned by Satan, to ensure the will of God was resisted.

Daniel was unaware of the invisible warfare that raging over the entire region. Principalities spirits exercise great power, authority, and influence over a land, community, or territory because wherever Satan assigns them, they exercise their territorial authority there. But God sent Michael, one of the chief princes as reinforcement to withstand the prince of Persia. We must pray for those in authority. First Timothy 2:1-2 (NLT) encourages us: "I urge you, first of all, to pray for all people. As you make your requests, plead for God's mercy upon them, and give thanks. Pray this way for kings and all others who are in authority, so that we can live in peace and quietness, in godliness and dignity." If a principality spirit is assigned over an individual or a community, it will resist the will of God and the advancement of the kingdom of God there.

This is one reason churches don't grow in a particular community. Principalities spirits are there to enforce the will of Satan over their territory. Take the focus off your needs, desires, and wants. There are souls who are dying spiritually because of rebellion and no peace. Pray that the Spirit of rebellion and religion will be broken over your territory. Pray that true salvation, deliverance, and the love of God will be released and restored over your region.

Destroying Evil Foundations

It is very important that we have the knowledge of foundations. Without this knowledge, many battles will be lost. Isaiah 28:16 (NASB) declares: "Therefore thus says the Lord, "Behold, I am laying in Zion a stone, a tested stone, a costly cornerstone for the foundation, firmly placed. He who believes in it will not be disturbed.""

We are in a fight and spiritual battle to possess the gates of the cities. This powerful promise was given to Abraham for his seed in Genesis 22:17-18 (NASB):

> "Indeed I will greatly bless you, and I will greatly multiply your seed as the stars of the heavens, and as the sand which is on the seashore; and your seed shall possess the gate of their enemies. And in your seed all the nations of the earth shall be blessed, because you have obeyed My voice."

Isaiah 11:3 (NASB) tells us: "If the foundations are destroyed, what can the righteous do?" The Lord will give strength to those who battle at the city gate. He told us that the gates of hell will not prevail. Gates symbolize authority.

"Raise your battle cry against her on every side!" (Jer. 50:15a NASB). Foundations can be heard. Micah 6:1-2 (NASB) says,

"Hear now what the Lord saying, arise, plead your case before the mountains, and let the hills hear your voice. Listen, you mountains, to the indictment of the Lord, and you enduring foundations of the earth, because the Lord has a case against His people; even with Israel He will dispute."

We need to build the waste places, and raise up the foundations of this generation. Isaiah 58:12 (NASB) declares: "And those from among you will rebuild the ancient ruins; you will raise up the age-old foundations; and you will be called the repairer of the breach, the restorer of the streets in which to dwell."

The church "having been built upon the foundation of apostles and prophets, Christ Jesus Himself being the corner stone" (Eph. 2:20 NASB). How do we wage war against an enemy? When enemies attack, you pursue them, killing and destroying what they rely on.

In First Samuel 30:8 (NASB) tells us: "And David inquired of the Lord, saying, "Shall I pursue this band? Shall I overtake them?" And He said to him, "Pursue, for you shall surely overtake them, and you shall surely rescue all." David was full of courage, fierceness, and his countenance terrified their adversaries.

Arise, Cry Out to the Lord

To cry out to the Lord is a fervent expression of faith in God and trust in His goodness and power to act on your behalf.

"Arise, cry aloud in the night, at the beginning of the night watches; pour out your heart like water before the presence of the Lord; Lift up your hands to Him for the life of your little ones who are faint because of hunger at the head of every street" (Lam. 2:19 NASB).

When you are in distress, call upon the Lord and cry out in humility, sincerity, and faith. Trust, lean, rely, and have confidence in Him at all times; pour out your hearts before Him. God is a refuge for us (a fortress and a high tower). He will fulfill the desires of those who reverently and worshipfully fear Him; He also will hear their cry and will save them.

The Bible is filled with examples of times when God answered the cries of His people and delivered them. Blind Bartimaeus called to Jesus, and He restored his sight (Mark 10:46-47 NASB "And they came to Jericho. And as He was going out from Jericho with His disciples and a great multitude, a blind beggar named Baritimaeus, the son Timaeus, was sitting by the road. And when he heard that it was Jesus the Nazarene, he began to cry out and say, "Jesus, Son of David, have mercy on me!""). He persisted despite his hindrances. Bartimaeus teaches us three things: persistence, faith, and gratitude. Despite how the people tried to silence him, he was persistent in getting Jesus's attention. He was healed because of his faith. Bartimaeus followed Jesus and gloried God.

Are you in need of a miracle? When Jesus stopped and called blind Bartimaeus to Him, he threw off his coat. Bartimaeus's coat represented his old way of life; it was his beggar's uniform and he was dressed for begging. If you're going to break out of your problems, you have to get rid of every burden. Lay aside every burden and every sin. Lay aside whatever is keeping you from putting Jesus first, whatever is holding you back from totally surrendering. Jesus is passing by your house, and this is your opportunity to receive your healing and deliverance.

Those who are thirsty for God to do something in their life, come out of the shadow. Enlarge your tent.

"Shout for joy, O barren one, you who have borne no child; break forth into joyful shouting and cry aloud, you who have not travailed; for the sons of the desolate one will be more numerous than the sons of the married woman," says the Lord. Enlarge the place of your tent; stretch out the curtains of your dwellings, spare not; lengthen your cords, and strengthen your pegs" (Isa. 54:1-2 NASB).

You must enlarge the place of your tent, in other words, expand your plans. Ephesians 3:20 (KJV) says, "Now unto him that is able to do exceeding abundantly above all that we ask or think, according to the power that worketh in us."

Increase your faith and shout. Mark 10:27 (NASB) encourages us: "With men it is impossible, but not with God; for all things are possible with God." Break forth and travail in your desolate region, where there is no sustenance of the presence of God, and without the joy of the Lord. Psalm 95:2-3 (NASB) inspires us:

"Let us come before His presence with thanksgiving; let us shout joyfully to Him with psalms. For the LORD is a great God, and a great King above all gods." The measure of your faith is not what you consume, but what you allow God to birth through you.

To shout or rua is to raise a shout, give a blast, war cry, sounding the alarm. It's time to raise your battle cry. Shout for the walls of the enemy are coming down. His foundation has fallen. The vengeance of the Lord will come upon him.

You are the chosen servant of the Lord. Isaiah 42:1 (NASB), "Behold, My Servant, whom I uphold; My chosen one in whom My soul delights. I have put my My Spirit upon Him; He will bring forth justice to the nations." This is an announcement of the servant of the Lord, and the work he will perform. The phrase "I have put my spirit upon him" means that God has qualified you for His work and office. Sing a new song to the Lord. Shout praises from the mountaintops. Isaiah's spirit was devastated, but God brought them revival. His love never changes.

Your Season Has Shifted

A tidal wave flooded with God's glory is about to hit your house. God has shifted our season to an "overflowing of abundance of blessings" watch God. What the devil meant for bad, God is turning around for our good. Stay focused with a positive attitude. A tidal wave of blessings is coming to the house of the Lord, especially to those who have stood the test of time. God is pouring waters of refreshment over your soul. Believe the Lord Jesus for the flood of increase, flood of healing, flood of breakthroughs, and miracles.

Psalm 42:7 (NASB) declares, "Deep calls to deep at the sound of Thy waterfalls; all Thy breakers and Thy waves have rolled over me." The devil wants you to feel depleted during hard times so that you do not rely on the promises of God. But through the eyes of faith, the kingdom of God is coming into alignment to help us overcome the obstacles before us because we have remained faithful and true to the divine call of God. Get into agreement with God. Paul prayed in Ephesians 1:18 (NASB) "I pray that the eyes of your heart may be enlightened, so that you may know what is the hope of His calling, what are the riches of the glory of His inheritance in the saints."

Doubters will believe again. It's canceling every attack and assignment of the enemy. Believers will be filled with the Holy Ghost. Habakkuk 2:14 (NASB) states, "For the earth will be filled, with the knowledge of the glory of the Lord, as the waters cover the sea."

Growth is coming to the kingdom of God. Psalm 72:16 (NASB) tells us, "May there be abundance of grain in the earth on top of the mountains; its fruit will wave like cedars of Lebanon; and may those from the city flourish like vegetation of the earth."

God is calling nations to holiness and righteousness, including the United States, China, Africa, Asia, the UK, Turkey, and Israel. Isaiah 60:1-5 (NLT) says,

"Arise, Jerusalem! Let your light shine for all to see! For the glory of the Lord rises to shine on you. Darkness as black as night covers all the nations of the earth, but the glory of the Lord rises and appears over you. All nations will come to your light; mighty kings will come to see your radiance. Look and see, for everyone is coming home! Your sons are coming from distant lands; your little daughters will be carried home. Your eyes will shine, and your heart will thrill with joy, for merchants from around the world will come to you. They will bring you the wealth of many lands."

The Way We Approach Jesus Will Determine Our Results

We have two situations in the two stories found in (Mark 5:22-25 NASB "And one of the synagogue officials named Jarius came up, and upon seeing Him, fell at His feet, and entreated Him earnestly, saying, My little daughter is at the point of death; please come and lay Your hands on her, that she may get well and live. And He went off with him; and a great multitude was following Him and pressing in on Him. And a woman who had a hemorrhage for twelve years"): the desperate and the hopeless. Jairus had a desperate approach which demonstrated four levels of faith: selfless, humble, pleading, and believing. The woman with the blood issue had a hopeless approach, which involved four frame of mind: the embarrassed, the expectant, believing, and the confessing. Hebrews 11:6 (NASB) says, "And without faith, it is impossible to please Him, for he who comes to God must believe that He is, and that He is a rewarder of those who seek Him."

Your attitude in approaching Jesus matters because, Isaiah 55:8 (NASB) declares: "For My thoughts are not your thoughts, neither are your ways My ways, declares the Lord." God sometimes allow delays, so you can learn more about Him. If you don't think you have this kind of faith, simply ask God to strengthen your faith. Psalm 46:1 (NASB) tells us: "God is our refuge and strength, a very present help in trouble."

It's Time for a Breakthrough

The Lord of the breakthrough is with us to break through on behalf of His people. He will give His people victory over those things that held them in bondage, and God's people will pass through the gates of victory. When the anointing came upon Cyrus found in Isaiah 45:1-2 (NASB) "Thus says the Lord to Cyrus His anointed, whom I have taken by the right hand, to subdue nations before him, and to loose the lions of kings; to open doors before him so that gate will not be shut; I will go before you and make the rough places smooth; I will shatter the doors of bronze, and cut through their iron bars."

The breaker anointing will remove hindrance, and delays. It unlocks the supernatural blessings. Micah 2:13 (NASB) says, "The Breaker goes up before them; they break out, pass through the gate, and go out by it. So their King goes on before them, and the Lord at their head."

We all face impossible situations that requires a breakers anointing. What is a breaker anointing? It is God's power to press through and break every hindrance and opposition that's blocking our supernatural breakthrough.

Isaiah 40:3-4 says: "A voice is calling, "Clear the way for the Lord in the wilderness; make smooth in the desert a highway for our God. Let every valley be lifted up, and every mountain and hill be made low; and let the rough ground become a plain, and the rugged terrain a broad valley."

The Lord is the Breaker who breaks open the gates, which held His people captive. Luke 4:18-19 (NASB) tells us: "The Spirit of the Lord is upon Me, because He anointed Me to preach the gospel to the poor. He has sent Me to proclaim release to the captives, and recovery of sight to the blind, to set free those who are downtrodden, to proclaim the favorable year of the Lord." Expect sudden and quick breakthroughs in your family, neighborhood, and nation.

The Choice Is Yours

The power to choose is a wonderful privilege and freedom. We win or lose by what we choose. You will know victory, prosperity, and abundance. We must choose who our real master is going to be, Satan or the Lord Jesus Christ: (2 Cor. 4:4 NLT "Satan, the god of this evil world, has blinded minds of those who don't believe, so they are unable to see the glorious light of the Good News that is shining upon them. They don't understand the message we preach about the glory of Christ, who is the exact likeness of God." John 14:4 NASB declares:"Jesus said to him, I am the way, and the truth, and the life; no one comes to the Father, but through Me"). The choice we make will affect our lifestyle and behavior. Too many Christians want to call Jesus Savior but will not allow Him to be Lord. The Christian life is a life of service and submission to Him who died for us. You win or lose by what you choose, whether victory or defeat, prosperity or poverty, and abundance or lack thereof.

Proverbs 8:34-35 (NASB) declares: "Blessed is the man who listens to me, watching daily at my gates, waiting at my doorposts. For he who finds me finds life, and obtains favor from the Lord."

This will be a season of alignment and positioning (2 Cor. 5:17 NASB "Therefore, if any man is in Christ, he is a new creature; the old things passed away; behold, new things have come"). Don't dwell on what went wrong. Focus on what to do next.

It's time to move forward. Jeremiah 7:23 (NASB) tells us: "But this is what I commanded them, saying, 'Obey My voice, and I will be your God, and you will be My people; and you will walk in all the way which I command you, that it may be well with you.'"

In this next season, we will have to use our princely authority to take dominion and prevail against the ruling principalities. There are benefits if you will just obey. John 4:37-38 (NASB) inspires us: "For in this case the saying is true, 'One sows, and another reaps. I sent you to reap that for which you have not labored; others have labored, and you have entered into their labor."

Our leader, the King of Kings, Lord of Lords, the Commanding Officer of the heavenly hosts, our General and mighty Man of war, has given us delegated authority over all the power of the enemy.

Satan and his demonic cohorts have the ability to oppress, possess, and terrorize us. Because Satan does not want us to serve and worship God. Ephesians 6:12 (NASB) declares: "For our struggle is not against flesh and blood, but against the rulers, against the powers, against the world forces of this darkness, against the spiritual forces of wickedness in the heavenly places." It is up to you and me to enforce that authority because "no weapon that is formed against you shall prosper; and every tongue that accuses you in judgment you will condemn. This is the heritage of the servants of the Lord, and their vindication is from Me, declares the Lord" (Isa. 54:17 NASB).

When we speak of the kingdom of darkness, we speak of any territory or domain where God is absent, along with His revelation, divine purpose, and destiny. Spiritual blindness is another one of Satan's weapons of mass destruction. In short, this an effective weapon because even if truth is presented, the blinded cannot see unless there is divine intervention through salvation, healing, and deliverance.

Second Corinthians 4:4 (NLT) gives us the reason for this level of spiritual blindness. It lets us know that "Satan, the god of this evil world, has blinded minds of those who don't believe, so they are unable to see the glorious light of the Good News that is shining upon them. They don't understand the message we preach about the glory of Christ, who is the exact likeness of God." Genesis 1:2–4 (NASB) says, "And the earth was formless and void, and darkness was over the surface of the deep; and the Spirit of God was moving over the surface of the waters. Then God said, Let there be light; and there was light. And God saw that the light was good; and God separated the light from the darkness."

Simple Act of Obedience

Obedience means to heed or conform to a command or authority. Most people are not desperate enough to do the impossible. However, faith will always require you to do something to activate the supernatural.

John 9:1-8 (NLT) tells us: "As Jesus was walking along, he saw a man who had been blind from birth. "Teacher," his disciples asked him, why was this man born blind? Was it a result of his own sins or those of his parents? It was not because of his sins or his parents' sins, Jesus answered. "He was born blind so the power of God could be seen in him. All of us must quickly carry out the tasks assigned us by the one who sent me, because there is little time left before the night falls and all work comes to an end. But while I am still here in the world, I am the light of the world." Then he spit on the ground, made mud with the salvia, and smoothed the mud over the blind man's eyes. He told him, "Go and wash in the pool of Siloam" (Siloam means Sent). So the man went and washed, and came back seeing! His neighbors and others who knew him as a blind beggar asked each other, "Is this the same man—that beggar?" This man was in need of a miracle. But the question is, how was he able to get to the pool of Siloam if he couldn't see? When you want something bad enough, your faith can activate supernaturally, allowing you to do the impossible without anyone else's help.

We have to stop making up excuses and follow the instructions of the Lord. One act of obedience can release a chain of miracles. Satan fights obedience. Obeying simple instructions releases the mighty power of miracles. It may not make sense to others, but the simple step of obedience may release the miracle that's right in front of you. We must choose to obey God in faith. Even when we don't understand it, it will deepen our relationship with Him.

Priestly Blessings

> First Peter 2:9 (NASB) tells us who we are in Christ: "But you are a chosen race, a royal priesthood, a holy nation, a people for God's own possession, that you may proclaim the excellencies of Him who has called you out of darkness into His marvelous light."

Priestly blessings are divine mandates, and their power is infinite and unrestricted. They can reach above and awaken the highest and newest divine desires so that their effect is felt immediately (Num. 6:24-26 NASB "The Lord bless you, and keep you; The Lord make His face shine on you, and be gracious to you; The Lord lift up His countenance on you, and give you peace"). The nation's portals have opened up to the prophets. A portal is a door, gate, or entrance to access something. Priestly blessings comes from the Lord. Psalm 24:5 (NASB) says: "He shall receive a blessing from the Lord and righteousness from the God of his salvation."

When the priests pronounced the words of the priestly blessings through the divine flow of the presence of God. Deuteronomy 11:13-14 (NASB) says: "And it shall come about, if you listen obediently to my commandments which I am commanding you today, to love the LORD your God and to serve Him with all your heart and all your soul, that He will give the rain for your land in its season, the early and late rain, that you may gather in your grain and your new wine and your oil."

We are directed to expect the blessings from the grace of our Lord Jesus Christ, the love of the Father, and the communion of the Holy Ghost. Second Corinthians 13:14 (NASB) says,

> "The grace of the Lord Jesus Christ, and the love of God, and the fellowship of the Holy Spirit, be with you all."

We who God has called should use our power and authority as leaders to promote the services of God, especially in the places where we live. Whatever is blocking your double anointing will have to leave. Haggai 2:9 (NASB) tells us: "The latter glory of this house will be greater than the former, says the Lord of hosts; and in this place I shall give peace, declares the Lord of hosts."

When you look and all you see are impossible situations, impossible conditions, and hopelessness, Jesus looks and sees a perfect opportunity for a miracle to display God's glory. Many times, what looks like a breakdown is just a setup for a breakthrough.

Pulling Down Strongholds

As a believer, you belong to the Lord Jesus Christ, we must stand firm on His Words: Ephesians 6:10-11 (NASB) declares: "Finally, be strong in the Lord, and in the strength of His might. Put on the full armor of God, that you may be able to stand firm against the schemes of the devil."

Strongholds are a mindset that holds you hostage. Sometimes the challenges of life in our brokenness, despair, and loneliness leaves us feeling that God has abandoned us. So we build a stronghold in our hard place. It becomes our fortified place of defense and security. Isaiah 41:10 (NASB) assures us: "Do not fear, for I am with you; do not anxiously look about you, for I am your God. I will strengthen you, surely I will help you. Surely I will uphold you with My righteous right hand."

These are three powerful weapons to use against the enemy: (1) Prayer–Psalm 26:2-3 (NASB) inspires us: "Examine me, O LORD, and try me; test my mind and my heart. For Thy lovingkindness is before my eyes, and I have walked in Thy truth." (2) Worship–2 Samuel 22:1-4 (NASB) tells us: "And David spoke the words of this song to the LORD in the day that the LORD delivered him from the hand of all his enemies and from the hand of Saul. And he said, 'The LORD is my rock and my fortress and my deliverer; my God, my rock, in whom I take refuge; my shield and the horn of my salvation, my stronghold and my refuge; my savior, Thou dost save me from violence. I call upon the LORD, who is worthy to be praised; and I am saved from my enemies.'" (3) The Word of God–Jeremiah 23:29 (NASB) declares: "Is not My word like fire? declares the LORD, and like a hammer which shatters a rock?"

Spiritual darkness exists where there is the absence of spiritual truth, not having fellowship with God, the mind and heart are darkened. Jesus says in Matthew 13:15 (NASB) "For the heart of this people has become dull, and with their ears they scarcely hear, and they have closed their eyes lest they should see with their eyes, and hear with their ears, and understand with their heart and return, and I should heal them."

Philippians 2:5-7 (NASB) tells us, "Have this attitude in yourselves which was also in Christ Jesus, who, although He existed in the form of God, did not regard equality with God a thing to be grasped, but emptied Himself, taking the form of a bondservant, and being made in the likeness of men." The last thing in the world Satan wants is a renewed mind, which produces a changed life.

Strongholds are built upon deception and lies, which the enemy uses to influence our thoughts. The word of God in 2 Corinthians 10:3-5 (NLT) says: "We are human, but we don't wage war as humans do. We use God's mighty weapons, not worldly weapons, to knock down the strongholds of human reasoning and to destroy false arguments. We destroy every proud obstacle that keeps people from knowing God. We capture their rebellious thoughts and teach them to obey Christ." The more the Lord Christ Jesus is the center focus of our thoughts, the less influence Satan will have over us. As a believer, discipline and examine your thought life by watching for satanic influences.

CPSIA information can be obtained
at www.ICGtesting.com
Printed in the USA
BVHW060738220321
603170BV00005B/1039